CONSERVATIVES IN POWER

BY EDWIN L. DALE, JR.

CONSERVATIVES IN POWER

A STUDY IN FRUSTRATION

DOUBLEDAY & COMPANY, INC.
GARDEN CITY, NEW YORK
1960

Library of Congress Catalog Card Number 60–5921

Copyright © 1960 by Edwin L. Dale, Jr.

To Todd
—who knows how to exercise the Fifth Freedom

CONTENTS

PART ONE

1   A Fork in the Road   11

2   Portrait of a Conservative   17

3   A Short Success Story   27

4   A Digression on Inflation   33

5   Onward and Upward with the Price Level   51

6   The Bounding Budget   61

7

CONTENTS

7 The Red and the Black   79

8 Of Money, Tight and Otherwise   93

9 Care and Feeding of the National Debt   107

10 A Final Thought on Inflation   117

PART TWO

11 A Tale of Two Slumps   125

12 Tampering with the Tax   147

13 To and From the States   157

14 Four Random Notes   167

PART THREE

15 Disengagement on the Farm   179

16 All This and Stagnation Too   195

17 Try, Try Again   205

18 The Sound and the Unsound   211

PART ONE

CHAPTER ONE

A FORK IN THE ROAD

ONE OF THE GREAT IRONIES OF THE ELECTION campaign of 1952 is that it was fought and won by General Eisenhower on essentially non-economic issues. The cumulative disaffection with the government in power—about the only thing that, in the end, can cause a change in regime—apparently stemmed from the Korean War, the alleged threat of internal communist infiltration, the loss of China, a few exposures of corruption, and, probably, a general sort of "anti-Truman" feeling. There had been full employment for two and one-half years before the election and, despite a sharp and classic rise in prices in the first year after the outbreak of the Korean War, price stability as well for nearly a year before the election. Aside from the old-line conservatives, who had never stopped feeling badly about Democratic regimes on economic grounds and were sure to vote Republican anyway, it is difficult to make a case that the Democrats lost the election of 1952 because of what was happening in the economy.

And yet it was a reasonable proposition before the election, and remains a reasonable proposition now, that if there are party differences in the United States at all, they are economic differences. If the Republican leopard turned out to have suspiciously Democratic spots in such matters as foreign policy and patronage, the economic philosophy, approach, and objectives of the Eisenhower administration have been different from its predecessors of the New and Fair Deals.

That difference underlies the question with which this book is concerned. The question, in brief, is this: What has the first conservative national administration in two decades meant in America? The related questions are obvious: Has it meant any really significant changes? What has a conservative administration, and the events under it, demonstrated about what government can and cannot, should and should not, do about the economic problems of the United States in the middle of the twentieth century?

The book is written late in the second term of the Eisenhower regime, in the conviction that enough has happened to warrant some assessments and judgments. The time span has included some events of considerable importance in American economic history; above all, it is a time span that has provided enough illumination, and enough detail, to sketch a revealing portrait of conservatives in power.

The story is in great part a story of frustration. The purpose here will be to examine the reasons for that frustration—with their lessons about our economy and the government's role in it—not to laugh at it. The common reaction in our society at the results of conservative economic policy has been, from the liberal side, to deride it, charge broken promises and still to object to the policy and its consequences; and from the still articulate and potent economic right, to charge a sort of betrayal. Both, I believe, are not quite fair.

There will be an occasional effort in this book to assess the validity of some of the conservative objectives and the policies aimed at achieving them, but that is not its purpose. I believe that on the whole they are perfectly valid and reasonable objectives, and they will generally be taken at their face value. The important story—and perhaps the tragic story—is the account of the obstacles that exist in modern society to the achievement of those objectives. Ironically, the conservatives themselves, in seeking the reasons for their failures, have often missed the truth—and with them, many of the rest of us.

Economic policy and action in this book will be taken

13

to cover the bulk of the administration's domestic policy. There will be not a word on foreign policy, including foreign economic policy. On the domestic side, such matters as civil rights, patronage and appointments, labor-union corruption, tidelands oil, and government "scandals" will also fall outside the pattern.

This line of demarcation has one great advantage and, possibly, one disadvantage. The advantage has been touched upon above: It is in economic matters that the parties, and the forces in society behind them, most clearly divide. There has been much talk in America about "the age of moderation" and the disappearance of deep divisions in our society. This is in part true. We do not have a Left as powerful and articulate as the Left in Britain, for example, and certainly we do not have the type of disaffected minority that brings large communist votes in France and Italy. We are agreed upon the essentials of our system; almost nobody seriously espouses "socialism" in the form of government control over the daily transactions in the economy or nationalization of the means of production. The "radical right," with its cry for abolition of the income tax and a general repeal of the twentieth century, is more a joke than a serious political force. But with all that, it is a great mistake to assume that we are rapidly becoming one big happy economic family. The differences are important—certainly in *objectives* if not always in results. America had a new regime when General Eisenhower was elected in 1952, and if anyone doubts it he need only look at the recommendations in the Economic Reports of the Truman and Eisenhower administrations (of which more later).

The possible disadvantage in selecting out economic policy is that, alas, economics remains as much as ever the dismal science. The problems of managing the national debt make, as my beloved grandmother once put it, "no detective story." The tribulations of Sherman Adams will be eternally more captivating than the trials of the Federal Reserve Board. There will necessarily be occasion in this book to make an effort, in an elementary sort of way, at explaining the economic facts and theories underlying certain actions, events, and policies. The reader is thus warned in advance. Fortunately, economics has the advantage of being, if no detective story, at least close to the bone of the ordinary man. Quemoy remains somewhat farther away than the price of bacon or the withholding tax or the availability of a job. One of the great, if somewhat ironic, contributions of the Eisenhower administration has been to make more clear the "dimensions of the possible" in modern economic policy—with implications for all of us.

A final word at this point. Despite the fulminations from the far and almost-far Right, there seems to me no reason to doubt that the Eisenhower administration has been a conservative administration in any meaningful sense of that word. To help win elections, and in part in a sort of act of self-delusion, it invented the term "modern Republican." It used phrases like "conservative when it comes to money and liberal when it comes to human beings." Now if "modern Republican" means acceptance of the basic changes in our society wrought by the New Deal—social security, legal protection of the right of labor to organize, a government role in housing and agriculture, bank-deposit insurance, and the like—then the term has a valid meaning. It was no doubt necessary to invent the term in order to persuade voters that the Republicans would not try to repeal the New Deal. The Conservatives in England did essentially the same thing. But the implications of the term very nearly stop at that point, with some relatively minor exceptions. At the fork of the road that was 1952—at the national point of decision as to what should be done *next*—the word *Republican* had more meaning than the word *modern*. America voted conservative: purposely or not, knowingly or not.

CHAPTER TWO

PORTRAIT OF A CONSERVATIVE

WHAT IS MEANT BY A "CONSERVATIVE" IN THE MOD-
ern American context? Whole books have been written
on this point without reaching much agreement. The
men who have guided the economic approach of the
Eisenhower administration—the main ones have been
Humphrey, Burns, Dodge, Folsom, Hauge, Martin, Anderson, Burgess, Saulnier, Weeks, Baird, Hughes, Brundage, Stans, Benson, and Mitchell[1]—differed markedly

[1] It is worth noting, incidentally, how few of these men were
businessmen, big or otherwise. Humphrey, Folsom, Weeks were all
in manufacturing, and Mitchell in retailing, but that is all. The repre-
sentation of bankers includes Burgess, Dodge, Baird, and Hughes. The
rest are scattered—including three economists (Burns, Saulnier,
Hauge).

17

on specific aspects of policy. Humphrey and Folsom were in close agreement on tax policy, differed on the propriety and extent of the "welfare state" and on the federal role in such matters as education. Burns and Saulnier were undisturbed by budget deficits if conditions called for them. Humphrey and Burgess felt nearly all deficits were bad. The editorial page of the *Wall Street Journal*—probably the most articulate expositor of the "classic" conservative position—felt the administration was wrong at least as often as it was right (though usually wrong in the sense of achievement rather than of objectives).

Yet out of this confusion of semantics and disagreement on a few specifics, a working portrait of the modern conservative in power can still be painted. The composite portrait bears a striking resemblance to the man who heads the whole outfit—President Eisenhower himself. This portrait is much more than a "lowest common denominator" of all the conservatives; on the essentials, I feel, the conservatives agree more than they disagree.

We shall have occasion in examining the conservative performance to elaborate in more detail some of the features of the conservative portrait and the reasoning behind the conservative stand. At this stage, the purpose is, by sketching the outstanding features of the portrait, to make clear that conservatives have a distinctly different view of the world and of government than do the liberals, and that the election of 1952 indeed meant a change. The conduct of political debate in America—and even more the writing of political party platforms —tends to obscure the degree of this difference.

The most striking feature of the portrait is a heavy stress on preserving the value of the money—stopping inflation (defined in this book throughout, incidentally, as simply a rising average level of prices). This may seem like favoring motherhood and virtue, but it is not. It involves very real choices in day-to-day decisions, and the conservatives have made, or tried to make, many choices that sacrificed something else of importance because stopping inflation was more important.

Many of the more intellectual Democrats and liberals generally—men like Leon Keyserling and Seymour Harris—are quite frank in saying that stopping inflation should *not* be the primary goal of American society. Working northern Democrats in Congress, while professing to be opposed to inflation, do not lose a great deal of sleep at night after taking actions—desirable for other purposes—that would tend to promote it. This Democratic position is quite honest, but it is not the position of the conservative.

In the old days the conservative viewpoint on inflation was considered the natural one of the "moneylenders" —Eastern bankers who wanted to be repaid in the same dollars that they had loaned. But after more than a decade of almost constant inflation throughout the

Western world it is quite clear that the position has more to it than that. Inflation hurts significant numbers of real people—even the relatively mild sort of inflation we have recently had in America. There are other reasons for the conservative view which we shall touch upon later. Suffice it to say at this point that a man of good will who has never been a "moneylender" in his life can conclude that a stable price level is better—if there must be a choice—than completely full employment or very rapid economic growth, or an extra safety margin in defense, or preserving small business, or desirable public improvements. He can make his decision on the old ground of the "greater good of the greater number." The conservative *performance* in this respect, of course, is another matter, and one of the major questions with which this book is concerned.

It is the primacy of the objective of preserving the value of the money that accounts for a group of associated features in our conservative portrait—emphasis on lower budgets, balanced budgets at all times except possibly in slumps when revenue inevitably falls off, willingness to employ high interest rates aggressively, efforts to "fund" the national debt. It is obvious from the mere listing that frustrations in some of these areas have been very great indeed. There is even some dispute as to whether stopping inflation actually requires these "classical" financial policies that are so prominent in the conservative spectrum. But at this point let us accept them as objectives which, if by no means peculiar to conservatives, are given much higher priority by conservatives than by liberals, and which, by all past tradition and almost certainly in fact, are essential in the task of preserving the value of the money.

The belief in the overriding importance of stable prices—together with the general conservative view of the role of the central government—also accounts for the manner in which the conservatives in power see and handle slumps in the economy. One point must be made at once: the modern conservative does not want slumps and painful unemployment, despite some foolish Democratic campaign oratory in 1958 to the contrary. There is no more of the "a little unemployment is needed to put the working classes in their place" type of thinking, at least not among the men who actually have been holding power. But the conservative does see the business cycle differently from the liberal in several important respects.

Without going into detail at this point, it is perhaps sufficient to say that the conservative feels slumps are quite normal events that usually tend to cure themselves. Thus his instinct is to avoid having the central government assume too large a role in curing them. Such a role would inevitably involve bigger deficits in the budget and thus run the risk of curing the slump at the price of more inflation later. The conservative tends to feel that inflationary remedies for slumps just make more and worse slumps inevitable. He constantly stresses the idea of *sustainable* prosperity, a rather vague term like "sound fiscal policy" but one which has meaning to a man like William McChesney Martin who is always using it. Has the modern conservative, then, accepted "Keynesianism"? We shall look into this matter at the appropriate place later. At this point, suffice it to say that he places far less faith in the ability of actions from Washington to achieve eternal prosperity than does his liberal counterpart, to say nothing of the fact that he is likely to oppose many of such actions as a matter of principle.

Let it not be implied from all this that the mid-1950's conservative is really no different from his mid-1930's father. He is markedly different. He accepts a federal role in the matter of the business cycle that would have seemed revolutionary even to Woodrow Wilson, let alone to Herbert Hoover. But for our purposes, the important point is that even in the matter of achieving prosperity and full employment—an objective common to the entire society—the conservative in power is a different animal from his Democratic predecessors.

The conservatives have another reason besides fear of inflation for their aim of lower budgets. This is their view of taxes. They feel that high taxes are positively dangerous to economic health, let alone being unpleasant. Equally important is their view of the *structure* of taxes. One of the two or three most clear-cut party-line votes since President Eisenhower came to power was over the big tax-reform bill of 1954, again to be touched upon later, in which the apparent choice was between tax changes to encourage investment, as proposed by the administration, and tax changes to encourage consumption, as proposed in a Democratic alternative. With taxes as high as they are now, the way they are levied makes a considerable difference. The conservatives in power reached perhaps their greatest degree of unanimity on this issue, though it came up only once in their regime because only once, alas, was there an opportunity to cut taxes.

So much for the financial aspects of the conservative portrait. Its other main feature is perhaps not quite as distinct, but the blurring of lines occurs less because of differing emphases among different members of the group in power than because of the essential slipperiness of the subject. This is the question of centralization of power.

In political sloganeering, the issue takes several forms —"states' rights," an end to "government competition with business," "freeing the farmers from the dead hand of bureaucracy," warning of the "controlled economy," etc. In a word, the conservative feels reluctant to have the federal government take on any new roles, powers, subsidies, etc., no matter how pressing a national need may seem to be; the liberal has no such instinctive reluctance. Here again, the frustrations and ironies have been great, but there have been some successes—at least negative successes—as well. Philosophically, this is perhaps the most important feature of all to the "bright young men" of the administration—a group centered in the new Department of Health, Education and Welfare and including such intellectuals as Arthur Larsen. These men were not quite so concerned about balanced budgets and stable price levels as they were with preserving what they call the "pluralistic" power structure in our society; they wanted not only the day-to-day workings of the economy but even the day-to-day workings of the "welfare state" to proceed as much as possible without interference and financing from Washington. They did not fear that the country was rapidly sinking into the horror of "socialism" under the New and Fair Deals, and they even backed a few new federal programs to cure specific ills; but they felt it essential for future liberty and future flexibility that the power of decision—economic and political—remain at least as dispersed as it was in 1952. They even tried, as we shall see, to abandon a few powers Washington already had. Their position, except in the case of new programs, was heartily backed by the more traditional conservatives centered in the Treasury and Budget Bureau.

To the conservative, "control" over the economy by the central government should be limited to *general* measures. For example, it is right, indeed inevitable, for the central bank to influence the total supply of money and credit, but it is better that private decisions of the private economy "allocate" this credit among competing demands. Thus the conservative instinctively resists a device like control of consumer credit, though in the end he may be forced reluctantly to accept it. He is convinced that direct government controls over individual transactions in the economy—price and wage control, and rationing—are bound to diminish rather than augment the general well-being. He is persuaded, in short, that a freely operating economy may allocate resources and wealth in ways that are sometimes not wholly desirable, but that an effort to allocate them from Washington is bound to be even worse. He may be as annoyed as the liberal at the relative place given by the American system to tail fins as compared with clearing up stream pollution; but he fears that an effort to impose a different allocation of resources presupposes a wisdom in governments that governments simply do not possess, to say nothing of his fear that such an expansion of the role of government is dangerous on grounds of power, taxation, and inflation. Thus in a very real sense, the conservative is opposed to "planning"—even the relatively tame version backed by what passes for an American "Left."

How sensible is the set of objectives revealed in this portrait of a modern conservative? We shall have occasion in describing actual performance to look more closely into that question, item by item. But I have no hesitation at this point in saying that there is nothing inherently retrograde or foolish or anachronistic about these objectives. When a conservative puts the desirability of a lower budget and "local responsibility" ahead of a massive federal program to clear slums; when he accepts occasional unemployment rather than perpetually pump up demand with probable inflationary consequences, he is making rational choices that can be defended and supported by large numbers of people outside of the New York and Chicago Union League Clubs.

Unfortunately, however, there remains the annoying gap in human affairs between objective and achievement. The story of why, on the whole, this gap has been all too evident in the years of conservatives in power is of course the story of this book. But the picture is by no means one of unrelieved failure. We might begin, then, by accentuating a bit of the positive—though it turns out to be a negative sort of positive.

CHAPTER THREE

A SHORT SUCCESS STORY

A CONSERVATIVE DESCENDING ON WASHINGTON IN January, 1953, could, and unconsciously did, divide things into two categories: things you don't do and things you want to change. Most of this book will be concerned with the latter. But the former is of no little importance. Indeed, in their "vetoes" the conservatives were on the whole successful. Before we start, in subsequent chapters, the study of frustration, let us glance briefly through the catalogue of success. It serves, incidentally, to sharpen the distinction between the 1952 conservatives and their predecessors.

How many people remember that Harry S. Truman

advocated a form of national health insurance—"social-ized medicine" if the pejorative term is preferred—in the United States? The fact that it got absolutely no-where in Congress does not change the fact that the national administration favored it. This was clearly beyond the pale to a conservative. The subject has scarcely been in the newspapers from January, 1953, until the present writing. The conservatives killed it.

Then there was the Truman threat to have the government build steel mills if the industry failed to expand on its own to the level of capacity that the "national interest" required. This was a very basic proposition—at the heart, if you will, of the "national planning" view of economic policy that is so dear to Leon Keyserling, Mr. Truman's economic high priest. It is violently at odds with the conservative philosophy and neither it nor any-thing like it has been heard of since 1952. To the con-trary, one of the first acts of the new administration was to sell the government-owned synthetic rubber plants. This issue has hovered at the fringes—and very quietly in the back pages—since, in connection with such items as government helium plants, oil-from-shale experi-mental plants, navy rope factories, and the like. The move, on the whole successful, has been toward disengagement and almost never toward expansion of the government role. To the extent "government com-petition with business" was important—which was not much—the Eisenhower regime diminished it a little.

A Short Success Story

Among the things conservatives don't do (many people who are far from radical wish they would) is to establish national standards for the unemployment compensation system, with an improvement and standardization of benefits by the states as a consequence. These conservatives didn't, despite considerable pressure in the 1957–58 recession and subsequently. Conservatives are also annoyed at plans to liberalize vastly old-age benefits under the social security system, partly because it means higher taxes and partly because it means some violation of the "insurance" principle whereby a man's benefits are related to his past earnings. They managed to block a number of proposals that got considerable liberal support in Congress, though benefits were improved modestly every other (election) year as usual during the six years, once with the active support of the administration.

Conservatives also feel that subsidized public housing, like a child, should be kept in its place. They did not kill the program already in the law but they had no regrets when Congress co-operated in their wish to keep the program at about 35,000 units a year instead of the 135,000 contemplated in the legislation enacted under Mr. Truman. Their position—not illogical—was that this seemed to be about all the nation's cities were prepared to apply for, and that it would be a great mistake to impose a huge low-rent program on the cities by *Diktat* from Washington. Until the 1957–58 recession the conservatives also successfully resisted persistent efforts to pump up private housing activity by the use of direct government mortgage financing. Even the billion-dollar program enacted in 1958 was strongly opposed and was accepted only because it was part of a package piece of legislation that the President had no choice but to sign. It has since been allowed to expire. The conservatives, too, managed to abolish that great symbol of the New Deal, the Reconstruction Finance Corporation, though they had to accept a compromise substitute in the form of a new Small Business Administration with reduced power to make loans to small business.

When Mr. Truman left office in January of 1953 he was convinced that price and wage controls, imposed hurriedly eight months after the Korean War had broken out, were still essential to prevent the pressures of mobilization from bursting out into a serious inflation. He had repeatedly urged Congress to strengthen the controls. He was quite wrong. The very first act of the conservatives in power was to wipe out those controls—mainly because direct controls, more than almost anything else, are anathema to the conservative view of how an economy should operate, but partly because they felt Mr. Truman's economic analysis was mistaken. Their success—for the moment—was complete. The Korean inflation had in fact spent itself, and the retreat from controls was carried out without losses.

In sum the conservatives quietly let die, or actively

blocked, a quite significant set of measures that had, and many of which still have, liberal backing. Now it is quite true that many of those measures sprang from Mr. Truman's brain without any sort of real communication with or sympathy from the men in Congress who would allow or refuse their passage. Indeed, the Housing Act of 1949 was the only major domestic reform enacted in the entire Truman second term. But this does not invalidate the thesis that the Eisenhower administration meant a change, nor does it invalidate the term "success" for its conservative efforts in this sense. Who knows what legislation might have passed, particularly in the 1959–60 Congress, if Mr. Truman were still President?

However, success in the category of "things you don't do" was relatively easy. It is always easier not to do something than to do it, and besides the leadership in Congress was co-operative—whether the Congress was nominally Democratic or Republican. It is, as mentioned above, the "things you want to change" with which this book is concerned.

The things the conservatives wanted to change formed an over-all pattern, with almost every item in the pattern connected with every other. None can be discussed wholly by itself, and none will be in the chapters that follow.

Fortunately, however, the items in the pattern—the

strands in the cloth, if you will—have enough identity to be extricated and put under the microscope by themselves, with the cross threads coming into view only as necessary. Yet the main cross thread—the one that cannot ever be pushed wholly aside—is the matter of inflation. We shall start the study of frustration with this issue because of its own supremacy among conservative objectives, because of its connection with nearly all of them, and because the frustration here leads naturally into an examination of the conservative performance with respect to the other items of the pattern.

CHAPTER FOUR

A DIGRESSION ON INFLATION

THE STATE OF ECONOMIC THOUGHT ON INFLATION IN modern America is at once exhilarating and depressing —the former because so much fresh thinking is being applied to a long-quiescent subject, the latter because, in a word, the doctors disagree.

Is inflation caused by "too much money chasing too few goods"—that is, excessive demand "pulling" up prices? Whole books are written to say that it is not,[1] while, conscious of the weight of tradition on their side, the defenders of this ancient and honorable doctrine

[1] E.g., Harold G. Moulton's *Can Inflation Be Controlled?* Anderson Kramer Associates, 1958.

confine themselves to articles and speeches and testi-
mony before Congressional committees. Have things
happened to the modern economy that render the
classic controls over the supply of money wielded by
the Federal Reserve System almost impotent? Again the
onslaught from the "new inflationists" (those who think
we must look for the explanation of our latter-day inflation in places other than the classic ones) grows ever
heavier, while governments all over the Western world
continue to act as if they thought little had changed.

Do labor unions cause inflation? The statistics fly—
often with the most flagrant manipulation—and there
emerges no certain answer. Do budget deficits? Yes, if
they are big enough, but there is no wholly convincing
answer to the question whether the kind of deficits we
have had from time to time in the past decade are a
significant cause of inflation. What of "administered
prices" or "monopolistic competition"—in short, concentration of economic power in big firms which are able to
maximize their profits by raising prices regardless of the
state of demand? Terms such as "unliquidated monopoly
gains"[2] are invented, knuckles are bared, the statistics
fly even faster—and still no good answer.

The search for possible culprits shows marvelous
ingenuity. Some experts point to the level and structure
of taxes, others to "excess liquidity." It is argued that
our technologically oriented society, with its vast pro-

[2] Coined by J. K. Galbraith in several articles.

liferation of new products and new processes, has added a basically inflationary fillip to the demand for capital goods of all kinds, even though the fruits of technology are more commonly viewed as the best possible way of improving labor productivity and thus cutting costs. Tariffs, farm price supports, sales taxes, insufficient savings, our shifting labor force—all have the finger of blame pointed at them, as important causes if not decisive ones.

It is literally open season on classic economic theory. A radical new interpretation of the money supply and its control[3] has been invented to account for what has been going on, and the experts are still digesting it. A group of economists of quite different political philosophies[4] have come up with the extraordinary idea that the best way to curb inflation in modern America is not to restrict demand (by the orthodox devices of budget surpluses and tight money) but to pump it up, on the ground that the rapid rate of economic growth and high output resulting from exuberant demand will cut unit costs and thus hold down prices; in short, the way to cure inflation is to inflate.

And in the wings rage three subsidiary debates: Is further inflation inevitable? Is "creeping inflation" (the kind we have recently had, and a very different thing

[3] John G. Gurley and E. S. Shaw in a series of articles in professional journals.
[4] E.g., Leon Keyserling, Richard Ruggles, and, in England, R. F. Harrod.

from the runaway inflations that are cited to frighten beginning students in economics) tolerable? Is a little inflation necessary to continued prosperity and economic growth, and therefore a small price to pay?

All of these questions—particularly those about the nature of inflation in modern conditions—have a great bearing on any assessment of the performance of the first conservative American government in two decades. The men in power believed, and acted in the belief, that modern inflation is essentially no different from what inflation has always been: too much total spending —that is, too much demand—in relation to supply. The way to fight it is to check spending by government, tax enough to cover what spending there is, and keep a firm rein on the money supply by using the powers of the central bank, with a consequence of high interest rates. The issue in the great economic debate is whether this theory, and its consequences for policy, is somehow outdated. While very few economists have gone so far as actually to reject the "demand" basis for inflation, many have felt that the newer forces making for higher prices from the "cost" side are so strong that they can frustrate the use of the classic weapons; it is a fairly common belief, for example, that if the use of these weapons to check demand is pushed far enough actually to halt the rise in prices, the consequences will be unemployment or, at best, a severe check to the rate of our economic growth, which depends upon a rising level of total spending.

It is obviously not the function of this book to attempt to resolve any of these questions, even if they could be resolved. However, it is a fact that the conservatives in power used the old weapons—or tried to use them—and failed to prevent a rise in prices of quite serious proportions. Is the explanation for their failure to be found in the fact that this was, after all, a "new" inflation not susceptible to attack by the classic devices for moderating demand? And if so, does this mean that we shall have to learn to live with an indefinite upward creep of prices on the order of 2 or 3 per cent a year?

In the context of the conservative problems and performance, I should like to hazard a few tentative conclusions that have formed themselves out of the maze of words and charts and statistics that cross a reporter's desk. The first relates to the batch of questions identified above as subsidiary debates taking place in the wings.

The conservatives, not only in the United States but elsewhere, have taken the unequivocal position that creeping inflation is *not* tolerable as a continuing condition. I believe they are probably right in their belief, and certainly right to take the position they do. It is not necessary here to go through again all the reasons why inflation is a "bad thing," with its impact on people of fixed incomes, etc. The more subtle, and perhaps more important, point is that a conviction on the part of the financially sophisticated public that inflation is inevitable could markedly change our entire investment climate (and has already shown signs of doing so), with great dangers for the future of our prosperity. If everybody buys stocks and nobody buys bonds, there is trouble ahead. Professor Sumner Slichter of Harvard, the apostle of the "a-little-inflation-is-quite-acceptable" school, is right, I believe, in saying that it will be a long time before the *general public* alters its savings and spending habits significantly because of creeping inflation. But a change in the habits of a relatively few people on Wall Street can make a big difference. We shall examine this point further in a later chapter.

One obvious corollary to that judgment is that creeping inflation is certainly not a necessary precondition for prosperity. Our past history has shown periods when prices were stable or even falling during periods of general growth and prosperity (and others when prices were rising). But if that record were not enough, there is the real possibility that creeping inflation—that is, uninterrupted slow inflation—is actually a threat to *sustained* prosperity. This would be the result mainly of the shifts in the investment climate mentioned above. We do not know for certain yet, but there remains the possibility that a widespread expectation of indefinite inflation will lead to the sort of speculative "bubble" that eventually gives way to a truly serious break in prosperity. Once again, my hesitant judgment coincides with the firmly held conclusion of the conservatives.

But is creeping inflation inevitable? The mainstream of present belief says "Yes," though there are important exceptions. The great irony, of course, is that the conviction of the inevitability of inflation did not fully take root until a conservative regime in America came to power and failed to stop inflation. Needless to say, I do not know the answer. But in any case, the answer depends in important measure on whether there are, or are not, significant new forces at work in the economy which escape the classic brakes available to the government.

It seems fairly clear to me that there *are* new forces in the modern economy making for inflation of a "non-classic" kind. They are usually lumped in the category of the "cost push," and they are not limited to the upward push of wages. For example, our technological explosion has meant, among other things, a drastic shift in the labor force out of pure production and into related activities, ranging from research to advertising and distribution, that are not susceptible of much mechanization. A white-collar worker is likely to be pure "overhead," and his numbers grow every year. Our tax laws work wondrous effects on costs and prices; this complicated field ranges from the effect of accelerated depreciation on costs of industry, to the direct effect on consumer prices of state and local sales taxes levied to pay for the enormous proliferation of works made necessary by an expanding population. But the most important of these new forces, and possibly the only one of any major significance, is the organization of labor into unions. In those sectors of the economy that are organized, unions can wield monopoly power over one vital factor of production, labor; and like all monopolies this relatively new one tends to raise prices—first the prices of the working people themselves (their wages) and then the prices of the things they make. Wages have almost surely risen faster in part of the postwar period than they would have risen in the absence of unions (for better or for worse), and they have certainly risen far faster than the productivity of labor could be improved by new machines and methods. My own belief is that the power of unions in the inflation sense has tended to be exaggerated, of which more later in this chapter. But it seems to me self-evident that *something* of an upward pressure on prices has been exerted from this source.

What of the "concentrated industry" problem (often misnamed the problem of "administered prices")?[5]

[5] As first defined by Gardiner Means, "administered" prices were merely prices that changed infrequently. More commonly, they are understood as prices that are set by the seller, as distinct from prices set by the free play of market forces of supply and demand. By this test, practically all prices have always been administered in the industrial age, the only important exceptions being farm prices and prices on the stock market. Buyers in America do not haggle; they pay the price listed by the seller. The key issue is not whether prices are

The more I read about this subject, the more convinced I am that it has little, if anything, to do with the problem of rising prices generally. The examples always cited are steel and automobiles, and there seems no reason to doubt that "pricing power" does exist in these industries and some others. That is, prices can be fixed, at least in the short run, almost regardless of the state of demand. But the greatest truth about the steel and automobile industries is the least known truth about them: Their importance for the economy as a whole is greatly exaggerated in the public mind. It has been calculated, for example, that the entire rise in steel prices since 1953 could have added directly less than 1 per cent to the consumer price index. Steel accounts for only 5 per cent of the "weight" in the industrial production index, and during the 1956 steel strike the gross national product—representing the economy as a whole—actually rose. There are three additional reasons why I do not believe the "concentrated industry" problem—whatever its implications in such areas as anti-trust law, economic power, etc.—has anything to do with "causing" inflation. One is that, while the statistics are elusive, there appears to have been no significant *increase* in the degree of

---

"administered" but the power of the seller to hold them or raise them in the face of declining demand. This power varies not only with the degree of concentration among the sellers but with the price elasticity of demand, substitutability of products and other factors. But it is clear that concentrated industries on the whole have more power over prices—more resistance to competitive price cutting—than other industries.

concentration in the American economy over the past ten years and possibly even over the past twenty or fifty. The second is the movement of profits. Until 1959, total dollar profits of American corporations in the 1950's had only once surpassed the 1950 peak. Profits have made up a declining share of the national income, and profit *margins*—the main key to prices—have, if anything, been declining as well. Without "excessive" profits, the whole administered price theory breaks down as an explanation for rising prices. It may be that the very big firms in concentrated industries can collect higher margins than others, but there does not appear to have been any big change in this situation in the modern period. Finally, labor costs constitute 60 to 70 per cent of the total cost structure in the economy and, on a purely quantitative basis, changes in wage rates are bound to mean more than changes in profit rates. While ducking to avoid the brickbats from the labor side, I should perhaps mention that the existence of "monopolistic competition" in some important industries probably does tend to weaken resistance to union demands in those industries, because higher costs can be readily covered by higher prices.

The important point about the general conclusion that new forces do exist in the economy is not that labor should be "blamed" but that governments have lost some control over the situation. Let me emphasize again that this point is still not settled; it could not begin to

be settled during the earlier postwar period because
"classic" demand forces for inflation were so strong in
the economy that no one could tell for certain whether
unions or other new forces were a cause or not. During
much of the postwar 1940's wages were obviously chasing prices upward, rather than forcing them upward,
and union-management bargains quite likely just rati-
fied a level of wages that would have existed anyway.
The experience of the post-Korea 1950's, while different, is too brief to be conclusive. But the smoke of the
"new inflationists" strongly implies a bit of fire. President
Eisenhower (with his appeals to "restraint" in press con-
ferences and formal economic reports) and the general
public (an 82 per cent majority in a late 1958 Gallup
poll thought rising wages a cause of higher prices) have
long since settled the debate in their minds. They think
private actions cause higher prices, regardless of balanced budgets or the money supply. If the theory of the
independent "cost push" as a cause of inflation has any
validity, as I believe it does, then *private economic
power* can operate to some degree quite independently
of the Government's efforts, almost all of which must be
directed to the limiting of borrowing and total spending—in short, demand. The first conservative government
in two decades came up against this new fact of economic life in a painful way.

However, the seriousness of this problem is another
matter. I feel, as will be noted, that it is on the whole

overrated. At this point, it is worth suggesting that the most undesirable aspect of the current structure of our economy and its costs may be the "ratchet effect": prices can go up but they can never come down. In the past there was nothing very strange about a mild general rise in prices during periods of prosperity, and a greater rise in prices during and immediately after wars. But almost always, certainly since the industrial revolution, prices (at least wholesale prices) fell most of the way back again when demand was sluggish and the economy went through its periodic slumps. In the postwar period in the United States this has not happened, except to a mild extent in 1949. The reasons are more complex than the existence of labor unions, with their power to prevent wage cuts, but that is an important reason. Another important reason is farm price supports. Another, hard to pin down statistically, may simply be changed ways of thinking and operating in the business community—a determination to avoid price cutting if at all possible, on the ground that nobody benefits (except the consumer). Whatever the explanation, the failure of prices in general to fall noticeably in three postwar recessions is one of the main reasons for the belief in the inevitability of creeping inflation, and for the corollary belief that demand has ceased to be the all-controlling factor.

What of the argument that "full employment"—and the commitment in law to maintain it—is the most important cause of inflation of them all? It seems quite clear that the existence of full employment over most of the postwar period, if it has done nothing else, has accomplished the "spillover effect"—the rise of non-union wages in such areas as the service industries to match or nearly match the increases won by the unions (though not to equal the *level* of union wages). This happened simply because labor was in relatively short supply. It is also clear that in our three postwar recessions, when employment was not so full, wage increases throughout the economy were a little less than when we had full prosperity, though there was scarcely a sign of wages actually falling as they used to do in slumps. In general, conditions of full employment imply conditions of vigorous demand, which alone can be sufficient to pull up prices, leaving wages aside. Yet the fact remains that reasonably full employment in the past has not always meant rising prices. In the modern context, it seems likely that "hyper-full" employment—I would put this at 3 per cent or less unemployment—will give an upward push or pull to prices, if sustained for any length of time. But the whole point of measures to restrain demand is to prevent employment (or anything else) from becoming "hyper-full"; there is no proof yet that we cannot have *reasonably* full employment (I would put this at between 4 and 5 per cent unemployed, with enough job opportunities opening all the time to limit the extent of long-term unemployment) with price stability. We had such a condition, for example, during most of the 1920's. During much of the postwar period unemployment has been less than this.

In this connection, it is worth recalling the idea, briefly mentioned earlier, that full employment, with its almost inevitable corollary of rapidly rising business sales and activity, is actually a *remedy* for inflation in the modern context. The idea is that costs, not demand, are now indeed the main upward force acting on prices. An economy operating with slack capacity tends to be inefficient; the work force and hence labor costs fall less rapidly than output, with the result that the cost per unit of output rises. Even if labor costs fall as fast as production, other costs of the "overhead" nature—local taxes, insurance, depreciation, advertising and selling expense, etc.—cannot, and once again the conclusion is that unit costs rise with falling output. Thus the remedy is to increase total demand by government measures, restore full employment and output, and count on a reduction of unit costs to curb the rise in prices.

There are, I believe, some flaws in this theory. For one thing, it appears to fly in the face of the fact that the three periods of price stability in the United States since the war, to be touched upon in the next chapter, coincided roughly with those periods in which demand was slack and unemployment at its highest. Some advocates of the new doctrine claim this price stability was not due to recession so much as to special factors, such as the movement of farm prices in the United States and the movement of import prices in Britain; and they have on their side some fairly convincing evidence that throughout the Western world the productivity of labor (the offset to the "cost-push" effect of higher wages) has risen fastest when the economy was booming. The argument is far from settled, but in our context it is important to note that a high level of employment *can* work both ways: it augments the tendency of wages to rise, but it probably also increases efficiency and productivity as well, thus moderating the effect of those higher wages. Once again, the conclusion is that reasonably full employment need not, per se, make inflation inevitable.

But that leaves the question, to which we now return, of whether the upward cost push, largely created by the economic power of organized labor, is enough to cause a constant rise in prices, no matter what governments do to keep demand from becoming excessive and no matter how much, within reason, productivity rises. Without this problem, it would appear that the prevention of inflation would involve handling the budget and the money supply in such a way as to keep the economy prosperous and growing, but not *too* prosperous and not growing *too* fast. In short, the remedy would, after all, be in the use of the classic weapons in an effort to prevent a condition of "too much money chasing too few goods." I have suggested that I believe the independent cost-push problem *can* partly frustrate this ideal achievement.

But—and this may be the most important point of all—there is an enormous difference between an average inflation of 1 per cent a year for ten years and an inflation of 3 per cent or more a year over the same period. In the first case a savings bond worth $100 would lose only $10 of its value, in the second $30. In the first case, decisions of people and investors might very well be made as if no inflation existed; in the second they would certainly be made in the consciousness of inflation. My own belief is that this central difference—small in a year but very large in a decade—comes close to resolving the great debate about the "new inflation." I am reasonably well convinced that the new private economic power, our tax system, our shifting labor force, and all the other non-demand factors making for higher prices cannot cause a very large inflation—a 3 per cent average inflation—unless the government's measures relating to demand permit it. For one thing, only one-third of our non-farm labor force is unionized. An enormous proportion of the prices we as consumers actually pay and worry about have nothing, or very little, to do with the much-publicized wage settlements in the steel or automobile industries—medical care, for example, or most important, food. For another, the cost-push (and demand-pull) effects of our technology have their offsetting counterpart in improved productivity, with consequent reduction in costs. Most important of all, it is abundantly clear that the really serious inflations that have afflicted various nations in this century—from Germany in the 1920's to Chile and Brazil in the 1950's—have been completely classic: huge budget deficits, resort to the "printing press," etc.

My hesitant conclusion, then, is that the classic explanation of inflation—excessive demand—is not only not dead, but probably remains the most valid explanation of them all. And this leads to the conclusion that the chief reason for the conservative frustration in the achievement of the most important of their objectives—curbing inflation—was not a result of their reliance on old weapons in a new world.

With a word of sympathy, then, at the task of *any* government in stopping inflation altogether in the new climate, on to the story of what actually happened and wherein, and to what extent, the conservatives failed.

CHAPTER FIVE

ONWARD AND UPWARD WITH THE PRICE LEVEL

INFLATION—RISING PRICES—HAS NOT BEEN A VIRTU-ally perpetual condition in America, contrary to general belief. From shortly after the Civil War until about 1890 prices were in a long drift downward, interrupted occasionally by short-lived increases during booms. They rose almost equally steadily for the fifteen years prior to World War I, partly, it seems, because the world was flooded with new gold during that period and there did not exist modern instruments to offset the inflationary effects of the gold on the money supply. After a typical sharp spurt during and immediately after World War I, prices fell back again much of the way in the early 1920's and then remained generally stable until the Great Depression, when they moved sharply downward. Inflation is by no means a condition peculiar to modern times, but neither is it something of the order of a law of nature. Prices over long periods of time, both in theory and in practice, can remain stable even as wage levels gradually rise, because of rising productivity—the effect of machines on the output of each worker per man-hour.

During but mostly after World War II there was again a typical wartime inflation, delayed in its manifestation by the wartime price and wage controls. The money supply was expanded enormously as the government paid for the war in large part out of "printing-press" money, as invariably happens. Few economists were surprised when this great increase in money in the hands of people and businesses spent itself in a big surge of prices from 1946 to 1948. One of the more flagrant distortions of fairness that occur in political debate has been the Republican habit of including those years in the "Truman inflation" and coming up with fantastically large percentages for the rise in prices under Mr. Truman.

Then for just under two years, from late 1948 to mid-1950, prices were stable. Much of this period coincided with the mild 1949 recession, but it was the fairly general belief that postwar "normality" had probably arrived. Then came Korea and a very sharp and sudden rise in prices again—also, incidentally, included in the "Truman inflation." It seems fairly clear that the Truman administration made some mistakes during the 1946–52 period—in particular the mistake, up to 1951, of refusing altogether to use the weapon of controlling the money supply by Federal Reserve action ("tight money"). But it is equally clear that the great bulk of the 50 per cent rise in prices from 1945 through 1952 was war-related. And war-related, incidentally, means demand-related: there was literally too much money chasing too few goods.

Although inflation was one of the war cries of General Eisenhower in the 1952 campaign, in fact consumer prices had again stabilized about the middle of 1952, wholesale prices somewhat earlier. This stability lasted for nearly four years (years that included the 1953–54 recession). The real tragedy of the conservative regime was that all the major conditions for price stability seemed to be present—no war, no "hangover" in the form of a large preceding rise in prices, and no ideological impediment to the use of the government's classic anti-inflation weapons—and yet prices began rising again.

Let us be clear at once that the inflation after 1955 was no piddling thing. True, it was not as steep as either of the two earlier postwar inflations. But neither was it a "creep" so slow as to be almost unnoticeable. Consumer prices between March of 1956 and March of 1958 rose 7.5 per cent—a rate that would cut the value of the dollar in half in less than fifteen years. Wholesale prices did the same, though the rise began earlier and stopped earlier.

A great deal has been made of the movements of individual prices, and individual sectors of prices, during both the period of stability and the subsequent period of inflation. Gardiner Means, for example, has stressed the fact that the great bulk of the rise in wholesale prices during this entire period was accounted for by increases in the concentrated ("administered" price) sectors, and it is certainly true that the price of steel rose consistently year by year. While prices were stable in 1953, 1954, and most of 1955, Democrats in Congress never tired of saying that this was a "phony" stability in the averages, with a decline in farm and food prices offsetting an increase in prices of "everything else." Later, more and more stress was attached, in the consumer area, to the persistent rise in the price of services, ranging from haircuts to rent, from auto insurance to local transit, from medical care to TV repair—none of them, incidentally, involved in the "big business" and "big labor" part of the economy.

And yet for every effort to demonstrate that these variant movements proved something artificial about the stability or unique about the inflation, there was an offsetting answer. To the charge that "administered" prices dominated the 1955–58 wholesale price inflation there came the riposte that the heavy-goods sectors, where concentration of industry is greatest, were precisely the areas where demand was heaviest in that period—a period, among other things, of boom in capital investment by industry. If one talked of consumer prices, one could not account for the stability in prices from 1952 through 1955 by the drop in food prices alone, for consumer durables generally—influenced by the emergence of discount houses—were also declining (in spite of the rise in steel prices); indeed services were about the only items at the *consumer* level that were rising. Later, when consumer prices started to go up, the rise was surprisingly general, with food and goods— both durable and non-durable—joining services.

Most of all, there are two impressive reasons for doubting that the diverse movements of different groups of prices proved that this inflation was somehow not a "real" or classic inflation at all. One is that there has seldom been a time when *all* prices moved the same way. Barring wartime and its immediate aftermath, the common condition of an industrial society is for some prices to be declining while others are rising, usually reflecting either differing states of demand for the items involved or differing possibilities of offsetting labor costs through higher productivity. Haircuts, with limited possibilities of mechanization, may go on rising indefinitely, but that will not necessarily be "inflation." The second reason is that no general rise in average prices can occur unless there is enough aggregate money demand to "ratify" or "validate" it. If inflation in the 1955–58 period did not seem to be characterized by "too much money chasing too few goods" (there certainly were few actual shortages during most of this period), it was very definitely characterized by "enough money to chase the available goods even though their price was going up"—in short, an excess of total demand above that required by a stable price level.

In any case, starting in mid-1955 for wholesale prices and March of 1956 for consumer prices, practically everything started to go up (and services continued to go up). My cautious conclusion, as I have suggested, is that it was a fairly "normal" inflation. By the time it stopped—in early 1957 for wholesale prices and in mid-1958 for consumer prices—the dollar had lost eight cents of its previous value, and it took a sharp recession to halt the rise. The American consumer was learning to live with a new, and higher, price level. The conservatives had failed in probably the most important objective they had.

What happened? As we have noted in the last chapter and in this one, the experts are not entirely sure. Indeed, it was the 1956–58 inflation that in great part gave rise to the renewed debate on this intricate subject. The main reason for the questioning and analyzing is that, on the surface at least, the government was wielding the classic anti-inflation weapons as it should, yet prices rose anyway.

The two principal weapons, as we have briefly indicated, are the budget and Federal Reserve monetary policy. The budget had a small surplus in fiscal years 1956 and 1957—that is from mid-1955 to mid-1957, the very time when prices were rising. The Federal Reserve began tightening money in early 1955, and by the summer of 1957 it had helped push interest rates to levels not seen since pre-depression days. As a corollary, the Federal Reserve action kept the expansion in the money supply to extremely modest proportions—a smaller rise, in fact, than would normally be necessary to allow for growth of the economy. The third weapon, management of the national debt, could not be brandished effectively after about mid-1956. But still, a traditional-minded and quite courageous conservative government appeared to be doing what governments are supposed to do to stop inflation, and yet prices went merrily upward.

In part, of course, the price rise was a quite normal counterpart of a period of prosperity. In part, no doubt, it reflected the "new" forces in the economy discussed in the last chapter; certainly the new forces had something to do with the failure of the 1956–58 increase in prices to be reversed during the subsequent slump. But neither of these things is quite enough to explain the apparent paradox—given the belief that the classic forces of demand are still the key to *serious* inflation—that prices were going up this fast in 1956 and 1957 while the government appeared to be performing as it should.

Fortunately, there is an explanation. It is that the surface picture of the use of the government's weapons is a somewhat misleading one. For the fact is that, for one reason or another, the conservatives were not really using the classic weapons with much force at all. Whether they should be blamed for this is another question which will be examined in the next four chapters. But the key point now is that nothing in the experience of 1956–58 really refuted the idea that inflation can be kept within reasonable bounds by "classic" government actions to restrain demand. The balanced budget was not what it seemed, and neither was tight money. The conservatives, in considerable part, failed because they did not, or were unable to, use their own pet weapons.

At this point it is necessary to do a mildly complicated exercise in the chicken and the egg.

We have four "things" to deal with: the budget, monetary restraint by the Federal Reserve, management of the national debt, and inflation. They are all related—*but in reciprocal directions*. All of the following statements are true:

> A bigger budget tends to make inflation worse and inflation makes a bigger budget.

   Tight money sometimes makes anti-inflationary debt management more difficult, yet "inflationary" debt management makes tight money more difficult to carry out.
   A bigger budget tends to thwart the effects of tight money, yet tight money (by raising the interest cost on the national debt) makes budgets bigger.
   Anti-inflationary debt management is possible only when there is no inflation.

This looks like an impossible series of dilemmas, and in part that is the case. There *are* some inherent dilemmas in using the classic government financial controls over the economy. But the main dilemma can be summed up in one sentence: The existence of inflation, given our modern financial structure, makes the use of anti-inflation weapons more difficult. Practically every government in the free world has made this discovery.

We shall take a look at each of the three main weapons and how the conservatives used them. The point to note here is that in part the frustration—the failure to prevent inflation—occurred because of this problem. Once the inflation started, probably in normal response to the generally booming condition of the economy, the job of stopping it became progressively more difficult until at last it evaporated in a very sharp recession with over five million men and women out of work during part of 1958.

This set of financial paradoxes *is*, without much

doubt, a new force in our economy. It arises from two things that no one will dispute are peculiar to the modern world—big budgets and a big national debt. Neither were or are the fault of the Eisenhower conservatives.

This dilemma, like the existence of new forces such as labor unions in the economy, made the job of the conservatives more difficult and is part of the story of frustration. It will be described in more detail in the next few chapters. But it is not the whole story. The difficulties imposed by the nation's new financial situation were compounded by others mostly not of the making of the men who came to Washington in 1952. On, then, to the story of Eisenhower finance.

CHAPTER SIX

THE BOUNDING BUDGET

ON A COLD JANUARY DAY IN 1957 GEORGE MAGOFFIN Humphrey, the ebullient, strong-willed Secretary of the Treasury who had symbolized Eisenhower economic policy in the first four years of the regime, suddenly blew his top. To the enlightenment of the citizenry, he did it in public—at a press conference held in connection with the transmission of the fiscal 1958 budget. Mr. Humphrey said that if the upward trend revealed in that budget continued for long, the United States was bound to have "a depression that will curl your hair." To put it mildly, he was upset.

The extraordinary Humphrey incident—a Secretary

of the Treasury exploding at his own administration's budget—was, of course, the very epitome of the frustration of the conservatives in power. If George Humphrey did not like the size of the budget, people asked, why didn't he do something about it? If the reply was that the budget was not Mr. Humphrey's direct responsibility, the counter-reply was that the Director of the Budget—then Percival Brundage—was no happier about it than George Humphrey. And the next year, despite Mr. Humphrey's horror, things were to get even worse.

What strange world, then, was this? Wasn't the budget at the heart of an administration's policy—the very expression of what it wanted to do? This chapter will deal with that question. The answer, though familiar to a few experts, is not generally realized by the public. But first, let us take a closer look at why conservatives care as much as they do about the size of the budget.

When Vice-President Richard Nixon was trying in the early fall of 1958 to induce wealthy Republicans to loosen their purse strings for the campaign of that year, he discovered that their major complaint—and their major disillusionment with the conservative administration they had so fervently desired—was over the size of the budget. It had by then risen to a peacetime record of about $80 billion (the estimate for fiscal year 1959, ending June 30, 1959) on a conventional accounting basis, and a good deal more (about $94 billion) on the more meaningful cash accounting basis. This was in contrast with a hopeful pledge by General Eisenhower in his first campaign to aim for a $60 billion budget on the conventional basis. It was a rise in four years of $16 billion in the conventional budget and $24 billion in the cash budget, which includes items like highways, social security, and unemployment compensation that are financed by "trust funds." The unhappiness of the wealthy Republican contributors was understandable.

Why should they care so? Does the size of the budget really matter that much? Or is the conservative emphasis on this point just a reflection of a visceral feeling carried over from the past with little rational validity?

The answer is that the size of the budget *does* matter, though the alleged danger of any given size of budget is obviously open to debate. Conservative, middle-of-the-road, and even left-wing governments all over the world have been grappling with runaway budgets ever since the modern economic era dawned after World War II. No less an institution than the impartial and undoctrinaire International Monetary Fund, in its endless quest for world economic stability (which means, among other things, a fair degree of price stability) has laid great emphasis on what the economists call "fiscal policy"—meaning in this context holding spending under control and covering what spending there is by taxation. The famous, and overworked, Republican cry for a "sound fiscal policy" has a genuine meaning.

We have already mentioned briefly the two major reasons why the size of the budget is important to a conservative, and we shall examine them a bit more closely here.

The first is simply that big budgets, all other things being equal, tend to be inflationary. This is almost certainly true *even if spending is covered by taxes*—that is, even if the budget is balanced. The question of deficits will be touched on later, and it is clear that a given budget is much more inflationary if it shows a deficit than if it is balanced. But economists are coming more and more to a view that can be stated as follows: In an economy of a size (as measured by the gross national product) of, say, $450 billion, federal spending of $80 billion is likely to give an upward pull to the price level where federal spending of $20 billion would not, regardless of the amount of revenue. The point is being debated among the experts, particularly as to degree, but there seems little doubt of its basic validity.

A big cause of this effect is fairly obvious. The idea that a balanced budget, no matter how big, will not be inflationary is based on the proposition that a dollar of private spending will be subtracted, by taxes, for every dollar of public spending that is added. But in fact all of that money raised in taxes would not have been spent; some of it would have been saved. Whether this saved money would in turn have found its way into the spending stream via investment depends upon the state of the economy and other factors, but in general it seems clear that an addition to public spending almost always makes some net addition to the total spending stream.

All of this is particularly true, of course, when the economy is booming and generating its own inflationary pressure (as was true in 1956 and 1957). A big budget in a slump can be positively desirable, because that is the time when more, rather than less, total spending is needed. But then, in theory, the desirable increase in the budget during a slump should be offset by reductions later during prosperity.

The second major reason why the size of the budget is important to a conservative is that, to minimize the inflationary effect described above, the spending must be covered by taxes. *Ergo*, big budgets mean high taxes. Conservatives have a special cause for disliking high taxes, quite apart from the fact that nobody likes them and that conservatives, on the whole probably a bit richer, pay more than a proportionate share. Behind their deep distaste is their belief that high taxes act as a serious brake on economic progress. It was this thought that raised for George Humphrey the specter of future depression.

High taxes are said to discourage incentives, to distort economic "energy" into non-economic pursuits, to "dry up risk capital," to deter investment in the plant and equipment needed to create new jobs, and a number of other dreadful things. Whether they in fact do so is the subject of an endless and perhaps a little tiresome debate. The figures, as usual, are susceptible of being used to serve the purposes of the debater, and the evidence is in any case mixed. It is reasonably clear, of course, that present tax rates in America have not been high enough to do any major damage so far to our growth and progress; otherwise we should not have grown as much as we have in the postwar period, nor should we have been able to achieve the extraordinary rate of $37 billion investment in new plant and equipment at the peak of the 1955–57 boom. Still, my own belief is that the conservative view is not without merit. There is a point above which taxes obviously hurt the economy, and Britain may be the best recent example of it.

So much for the conviction—a respectable conviction —that big budgets are bad. But what of the constant series of expert analyses to the effect that the United States can easily "afford" a much higher level of government spending, on defense or on other things? This concept is, in part, a semantic trick, just as the conservative claim that "a sound economy is the first essential of a sound defense" is a semantic trick. What is meant by "afford" and what is meant by "sound economy"? Those who say we could spend much more mean that if we did our economy would not "collapse" (economies almost never do), that the sacrifices which might result in the form of higher taxes or higher prices, or both, would be small in relation to the benefits of the higher spending. That may be quite true. But the fact remains that there is almost surely a real cost in higher budgets. When the conservative talks about a "sound economy" he means an economy with the present or lower tax rates and a stable price level (he really means a *desirable* economy, in his terms). The United States, the dark fears of Senator Harry Byrd to the contrary notwithstanding, would not suffer any disasters from higher budgets than we have, but in several important respects it would be a worse place to live: both taxes and prices would quite likely be higher, and, depending on where the money was spent, one level of well-being and even our economic growth might well be lower.

It ought to be mentioned at this point that, even granting the conservative position, the size of the budget can be viewed sensibly only in relation to the size of the economy. For one thing, as the economy grows— meaning higher incomes, more profits, and more transactions all around—a given set of tax rates raises more revenue. Thus federal spending can rise gradually over time without any increase in taxes (though of course, as a conservative would quickly note, if spending always rises taxes cannot be cut, either). For another thing, what inflationary effect there is in high federal spending per se is less as the size of the budget in relation to the economy is less. There is little doubt that Americans of the next generation will view with equanimity—and properly so—budgets of more than $100 billion. But there will still be an important difference between a 1975 budget of $100 billion and one of $120 billion. Looked at from any angle, the increase in federal spending from the Eisenhower low of $64.6 billion in fiscal 1955 to over $80 billion in fiscal 1959 was so large and so rapid that Mr. Nixon's reluctant Republicans had every reason to feel as they did.

In examining later the question of balanced and unbalanced budgets, we shall trace the early movements of the budget, before 1955. The point at issue here is how the subsequent enormous increase came about. How did the conservatives fail so badly in this central aspect of their doctrine? The answer to this question is of great importance to future American governments and to the future of the economy. There are five—and only five—important parts to the answer, some familiar and some not so familiar.

1. *Inflation*. This must be mentioned first because it affects all the others. It cannot be exactly quantified, of course. How much less would the same amount of defense have cost if there had been no post-1955 inflation? How much less would federal salaries have had to be raised? How much less increase would there have been in various welfare payments partly financed from Washington?

But if no precise dollar figure can be put on this item, there is one rough measure. The national income accounts contain one of those ghastly economists' terms called "implicit price deflater for government income and product account." It is a measure of the increase in prices for the goods and services (including the services of its own employees) that the government buys. This does not cover by any means all government spending, but it probably covers the great bulk of the spending that is most directly affected by a rising price level in the economy. It shows that between 1955 and 1957 the index of prices paid by the government rose from 103.9 to 115.7—or enough to add roughly $6 billion to the cost of the goods and services that the government buys.

This $6 billion shows up most particularly in the defense budget; that is, some of the rise in defense spending to be mentioned below is pure inflation. Next most important, it shows up in the pay of federal employees, which had to be increased as a matter of simple justice. That increase, obviously, is spread through every program of the government. Because the $6 billion covers only goods and services purchased, it would not find reflection in government benefit programs. But there is no doubt whatever that much of the increase in social security outlays (both those such as public assistance that are included in the regular budget and old-age insurance which is not) is accounted for by inflation. The increases in these programs voted by Congress, usually with the reluctant concurrence of the administration, were mainly aimed at keeping the beneficiaries even with the game.

We have mentioned before the chicken-and-egg problem involved here: Higher budgets tend to promote inflation and inflation tends to promote higher budgets. Mr. Humphrey discovered this, at some cost to his blood pressure. It was a truth not of his making but was inherent in the very fact of budgets that are large to begin with (the same inflation would have added only $1 billion to a $9 billion budget, the highest ever achieved during the New Deal).

2. *Defense.* It was, of course, not the fault of a conservative administration that defense technology should have accelerated at such a fantastic rate and that complicated weaponry naturally costs more than simple weaponry, quite apart from the effect of inflation. Nor was it the fault of the conservative administration that for the first time in history the American defense posture had to reckon with the possibility of immediate destruction of this nation.

The Republicans took office when the Korean War— and the steep mobilization curve of procurement that accompanied it—was about to end. Defense spending reached its peak of $43.6 billion in fiscal 1953, the last year of the war, and dropped quite naturally over the next two years to $35.5 billion in fiscal 1955, a level that was essentially unchanged in fiscal 1956. This can be said to be the "plateau" of peacetime spending on which the Republicans started. By fiscal 1959 the total was up to $41.2 billion.

Needless to say, the most common complaint about the Eisenhower defense budgets has been that they were too small—an issue beyond the scope of this book. A quite opposite complaint, gradually diminishing in intensity with rising hopelessness, is that there is too much "waste" in defense spending. Of course there is. But surely one firm conclusion from the first conservative regime in two decades is that nobody on earth can make the "waste" significantly less. The Republicans tried, and they had some small successes. But the fact of the matter is that no human institution can spend $40 billion efficiently, and we might as well learn to live with that fact. In my view, one of the most dangerous canards abroad in the land is the allegation that we could have the same defense for much less money if only the Pentagon were more efficient; it is dangerous because it leads to pressure to cut defense appropriations in the belief that only "fat" and not "muscle" will be affected.

Parallel with the increase in direct military spending —and resulting from essentially the same causes—was an increase of $900 million in atomic energy spending between fiscal 1955 and fiscal 1959. A little of this represented the new program of peaceful uses of the atom, particularly for power, but most of it was inflation and the need for more complex weapons. Thus, together, defense and atomic energy account for more than $6 billion of the total increase. It was an increase that obviously was beyond the control of the administration, though there is no doubt that administration decisions kept it from being even greater.

3. *Interest.* Here again the paradox. The conservatives quite rightly used "tight money" in the attack on inflation, of which more later. But one result was bigger budgets. The total expenditure for interest on the national debt depends on the size of the debt and the level of interest rates. In the period in question, the only important variable was the level of interest rates, the total debt being relatively stable. Spending on this item rose from $6.4 billion in fiscal 1955 to $7.6 billion in fiscal 1959, an increase of an impressive $1.2 billion, with worse to come in fiscal 1960.

4. *New programs.* There is a bit of trickery here. By all odds the most important new program launched by the conservatives was the big highway program, but they carefully shoved it outside the regular budget into a trust fund financed by highway-user taxes. In any real sense—the impact of the budget on prices and taxes —it should count. Highway spending rose from $650 million in fiscal 1955 to $2.6 billion in fiscal 1959.

But there were a few other programs, too. The most important besides highways was the very expensive program of modernizing the nation's civil aviation traffic control and communications facilities; the spending increase was from $250 million in 1955 to $570 million in 1959. There were substantial increases in expenditures for medical research (mostly, but not entirely, at the initiative of the administration), the aforementioned program for peaceful uses of the atom, space programs, a new program of small-business lending, a more aggressive use of the Export-Import Bank for rescue operations abroad, an expansion and modernization of the postal service so large as to count as a new program, a small program of federal assistance in the education field (to be touched upon later), and one or two others.

There should also be mentioned two temporary programs associated with the 1957-58 recession—a $1 billion mortgage purchase program that was one of the surprisingly rare cases of an item of important size pushed through on the initiative of Congress over the moderately vigorous protest of the administration, and a $400 million program of temporary, emergency unemployment compensation. Both were included in the $80 billion spending total of fiscal 1959, though they presumably will not recur.

I leave out of this list the soil bank, because its main effect was probably to prevent higher spending on farm price support, included in the next category. The total cost of the new programs launched by the administration is complicated by the special treatment of highways and the temporary nature of the two anti-recession programs. At a maximum, including everything, I would put it at nearly $5 billion by fiscal 1959. Including only budget items (thus omitting highways) and excluding the recession programs it would be in the neighborhood of $2 billion.

It seems to me to be so clear as to be beyond argument that every one of these new programs was either literally essential (civil aviation) or so desirable as to verge on the essential (highways, cancer research, postal improvement). When Brazil and Argentina were on the brink of bankruptcy, it was quite impossible to refuse to bail them out with the Export-Import Bank. Could the administration have refused to respond to the Soviet sputniks with a new space program? There was no conservative "weakness" in the approval of these items, as the *Wall Street Journal's* editorial page constantly implied. I would put it as flatly as this: With almost no exceptions, the conservatives had no choice.

We shall examine later the idea that "pressure groups" or the Democratic Congress forced on the conservative government things it did not want. For our purposes here, it is enough to say that to the extent they did, the amounts involved were extremely small, except for the $1 billion anti-recession mortgage program. In quantity terms, the increase in the budget from new programs came about because no government could possibly have chosen otherwise.

5. Here is the real *pièce de résistance,* the almost

unrecognized culprit for the conservative frustration. It can be termed the "open-end commitment."

This is a category of items of expenditure over which the government in power has absolutely no control, barring an almost impossible change in existing law. The initiative for the expenditure comes from *outside the government*, and the government has no choice but to put up the money. Of all our categories, it is by far the most frustrating.

The really appalling item in the list is the farm program. While Mr. Benson preached and schemed and basked in the approbation of city folk, the budget of his department rose from net spending of $2.9 billion in fiscal 1953 to over $7 billion in fiscal 1959. Between fiscal 1955 and fiscal 1959, the period we are considering, it rose by more than $3 billion. We shall have more to say of this in a subsequent chapter. The rise was by no means Mr. Benson's fault. It was nobody's fault, except possibly the makers of weather and fertilizers, and the members of Congress in 1938 who invented the program. But the figure is quite staggering. The *increase* in farm spending alone since the Republicans took office is more than is spent on the entire foreign-aid program, for example. And there was literally nothing the administration could do about it.

Three other items in this list of nightmares for the conservatives are worth mentioning.

One is veterans' pensions. This is distinct from

compensation for wartime injuries. It is a system under which any veteran of 65 or over is almost automatically counted "disabled" and, if he is fairly poor, gets a monthly pension. The veterans of World War I are now reaching 65 in increasing numbers, and the pension item has risen from $800 million in fiscal 1955 to over $1.1 billion in fiscal 1959. It will go right on rising indefinitely.

The next is that obscure little item in the welfare category called "aid to dependent children." When the father runs away, the mother goes to the local welfare department and qualifies for a special form of relief, partly financed by the federal government. Fathers have been particularly irresponsible under the conservatives, it seems. The federal share alone has risen from $355 million in fiscal 1955 to $615 million in fiscal 1959. The spending depends entirely on the number of people who apply and qualify.

The last is what goes by the name of "stockpiling." It is not going to be a continuing item, fortunately, but is cited here as illustrative. In order to induce expansion of facilities for producing aluminum and copper during the early days of the Korean War, the government had signed contracts allowing the producers to sell their output to the government if private markets weakened. Markets weakened starting in late 1956. The stuff was dumped on the government by the ton and spending spurted by an amount, not made public, somewhere upward of $100 million.

With the economic impact of the budget in mind, there ought to be mentioned at this point one of the greatest open-end commitments of them all—one that does not show in the ordinary budget figures because it is a trust-fund item, and one that certainly nobody begrudges. It is the old-age retirement system under social security. Payments here depend, of course, mainly on how many people retire and apply. They have gone up from $2.1 billion in fiscal 1952 to $4.5 billion in fiscal 1955 to $9.5 billion in fiscal 1959. Together with highways and the recession-induced spurt in unemployment compensation, these payments account for the fact that total cash spending rose $24 billion between 1955 and 1959 while ordinary budget spending rose "only" $16 billion.

At this point, a pause for breath. Is there any sort of pattern about all of this? I believe there is, and it is this: governments cannot control the size of budgets.

Now there are some important qualifications to this rather gloomy conclusion. Governments can, and the conservatives did, impose definite limits on the number of new programs started, for example. They can, and obviously do, make decisions in the area of defense that control the rate of increase in spending (though I am certain they cannot actually reduce defense budgets while the cold war lasts and the scientists germinate ideas).

But the basic generalization holds. It holds, ironically, even in rare cases when the trend of spending is briefly downward, as seems likely for fiscal 1960. This reduction did not come about because the conservatives willed it but mainly because the temporary anti-recession programs expired and a few other items, such as stockpiling, happened for reasons of their own to be heading downward. Each year in December the public is treated to a spate of newspaper stories on the new budget which leave the impression that the President is deciding how big the budget should be. He is not, except within very narrow limits. The basic size of the budget—whether it is nearly $80 billion or nearly $70 billion—has long since been decided for him. George Humphrey was frustrated because he found he could not control the one thing he thought he could control. It is not clear that Mr. Humphrey himself ever quite understood what had happened to him. He kept muttering darkly about "pressure groups" as the cause of his, and his administration's, troubles. Others, then and since, seemed to feel that the difficulty had something to do with the fact that a Republican administration was always bucking against a Democratic Congress—or more simply that all the blame should be laid to Congress. These two contentions, together with a few other aspects of Republican budget performance, will be taken up in the next chapter.

CHAPTER SEVEN

THE RED AND THE BLACK

WE HAVE EXAMINED IN SOME DETAIL THE REASONS behind one of the two or three greatest conservative frustrations of them all—the very steep rise in the federal budget from 1955 to 1959. It was a rise that almost certainly contributed its part to the 1956–58 inflation. But as we have noted, the influence of the budget on the price level depends not only on its size and its direction of movement, but even more on whether it is balanced. Here the conservative story appears a little less sad, at least on the surface. First, then, a brief look at the surplus-deficit story, and an important lesson it contains, and then we can return to a few final observations about budgets in the modern world.

Budget deficits, as even the more sophisticated conservatives will admit, by no means always need be inflationary. Whether they are depends on their size, how the necessary borrowing to cover them is done, and, most important of all, whether the economy is booming or operating with slack. A deficit in a slump, it is widely agreed among the experts, is a positive benefit. It is not inflationary in such times because, in effect, the federal government is borrowing and spending to make up for a lack of borrowing and spending in the private economy. An expansion of debt of one kind or another —private or governmental—is a precondition for prosperity and will not be inflationary unless it is excessive. In the United States since World War II, despite all the gnashing of teeth about deficits in the federal budget, the expansion of private debt has been far greater than the expansion of public debt. If, as some innocents have been known to advocate, the federal government conducted its affairs "like an ordinary family or business," the national debt would be perhaps twice its current size.

But with all that said, it remains true that no respectable attack on inflation can be conducted without a strong effort to cover government spending with government receipts, certainly in times of prosperity. "Balanced budgets," the phrase by which a conservative can always be identified, is overworked, but it has real meaning. The reason is simple: When the federal budget is in deficit, it is adding to the total spending stream, and thus adding to demand.

When the Republicans took office in January of 1953 they were appalled by what they found (if they had done more homework on how budgets work in the modern world, they need not have been). They found spending projected by the outgoing administration at $74.6 billion for fiscal 1953, then half over and not susceptible of change, and $78.6 billion for fiscal 1954, with deficits of $5.9 billion and $9.9 billion respectively. Times were prosperous, the Korean War was under way, and deficits were precisely the *wrong* medicine for the economy. Perhaps worst of all, the Republicans found a backlog of nearly $100 billion in appropriations voted by previous Congresses which were not yet spent—much of it committed in the form of orders for which deliveries of goods were still being awaited. With deficits in the immediate future unavoidable, one of the first acts of the new administration was to request of Congress an increase in the legal ceiling on the national debt.

The picture looked dark but it was not as bad as the conservatives at first feared. They found the Truman projections for 1954 contained a good deal of "water," chiefly in the form of new programs which were easy to eliminate. They were able to juggle the financing of a few programs, particularly in the housing field, to achieve a quick, though non-recurring, reduction in spending. Best of all, the Korean War ended in mid-

1953 and almost immediately defense spending began to trend downward of its own accord; this process was assisted by a freeze on major new defense commitments pending a "new look" that took a full year.

The results made the conservatives rather proud—though it is now clear that they counted their chickens much too soon. Total budget spending drifted down from the $74.3 billion of fiscal 1953, the Korean War peak, to $67.8 billion in fiscal 1954 and $64.6 billion in fiscal 1955. Things seemed to be well in hand.

Meanwhile, there seemed to be another reasonably good stroke of luck. This downward drift in spending would normally have meant early achievement of a balanced budget. The reason it did not was, however, a perfectly acceptable one: a mild recession in the economy began in mid-1953, with an inevitable effect on receipts. The conservatives willingly delayed the day of a balanced budget by further cutting receipts through a series of tax reductions in 1954. There was no serious problem in the resulting small deficits ($3.1 billion in fiscal 1954 and $4.2 billion in fiscal 1955) because the economy was operating with slack and inflation seemed no threat. With spending in check, the resumption of prosperity was bound to bring with it more receipts and a balanced budget.

It did. The budget showed a small surplus in both fiscal years 1956 and 1957, even though spending had then begun, slowly at first, its great rise. The conservatives had achieved one of their main aims, and to their credit this was only the second time the nation had had two balanced budgets in a row since before the New Deal.

But two points in mitigation must be made. The first is clear from the figures: It wasn't the government that "willed" a balanced budget but the prosperous economy, with its impact on receipts, that achieved it. Receipts rose, without any increase in tax rates, from $60.4 billion in fiscal 1955 to $71 billion in fiscal 1957. But the trouble with the economy is that it is unpredictable. In late 1957 it went into a sharp though brief slump. Before the conservatives could catch their breath their balanced budgets were out the window and they had, first, a moderate deficit of $2.8 billion in fiscal 1958 and, in fiscal 1959, the biggest peacetime deficit in history—$12.5 billion. The rise in spending that we have outlined played a major contribution in both, but the slump in receipts was at least equally important.

The second point is that the two surpluses, viewed in hindsight, were clearly not big enough to do the job surpluses are supposed to do—check the exuberance of the economy and thus temper the forces of inflation. They were only $1.6 billion in fiscal 1956 and the same in fiscal 1957. The reason they were not bigger, of course, was the rise in the spending side of the equation. But given this rise in spending, I suppose a case could be made that the conservatives, if they really wanted to attack inflation, should have repealed some of the 1954 tax cuts—in short, raised taxes. Such a move would of course have violated their other principle about the effect of taxation on economic growth. But the fact remains that the way "fiscal policy" fights inflation is to run big surpluses in booms; the conservatives, mainly because spending got away from them, ran only very small surpluses.

The huge deficit in fiscal 1959 was undoubtedly the crowning blow in the story of conservative frustration. It was far bigger than anything under either Roosevelt or Truman, except for the years of World War II. It forced the administration into the embarrassing position of twice having to ask Congress during 1958 for increases in the national debt limit, and again in 1959. Perhaps worst of all, it caused a disquieting reaction among the financially sophisticated at home and abroad. There arose for the first time the suspicion of a "weak" dollar, on the ground that American governments were incapable of controlling public spending and hence inflation. The shock to Robert Anderson, by then the Secretary of the Treasury, in discovering this during a foreign tour in late 1958 cannot be exaggerated. Whether or not the suspicions were warranted does not matter; what matters is that they existed—and existed as a result of what happened under a conservative American administration. In small part because of these fears, there was a huge outflow of gold from the United

States during 1958; that is, a few foreigners took "flight from the dollar" and converted their dollar balances into gold. More important was the threat that there would be a genuine "flight" if the situation ever got out of hand again.

Was the big deficit, however, actually the disaster that conservatives both home and abroad thought it? There was obviously slack in the economy during this period —a condition that, as we have seen, ordinarily should minimize the inflationary effect of deficits. It is quite clear that *some* deficit in this period was not only inevitable but positively desirable to help the economy out of the slump. Still, $12.5 billion is a pretty big deficit, even in relation to the huge size of our modern economy. Whether this deficit has, in effect, laid the groundwork for another burst of inflation later remains to be seen and is unproved at this writing. Suffice it to say that everyone in the government from the President down wished it were less, and that it has already contributed heavily to a wave of inflationary sentiment in the investment community.

The main lesson from this brief account is the enormous influence of the state of the economy on the red- or black-ink status of the budget—an influence that stems primarily from our heavy reliance on the income tax. Corporation taxes, in particular, gyrate dizzily with the slightest change in economic fortunes. Many economists would consider this sensitivity a good thing, on the ground that big deficits are just the right medicine in slumps. Others, worrying about the longer-term implications of deficits that are very large in slumps and apparently cannot be offset by equal surpluses in booms, are not so sure. In any case, for better or for worse, the famous goal of the balanced budget, it is now clear, depends in its crucial receipts aspect not on what governments want but on what the private economy does. The ironic truth for the conservatives was that even their one achievement—the two balanced budgets —occurred for reasons not of their making; the spending side of the budget was actually on the uptrend when the balance was achieved.

We can wind up the all-important story of the budget with a final word on our original theme. The account of the red and the black ink in the budget contains an important lesson about the movement of receipts in the modern economy, but the spending side of the equation remains probably the most significant—and the most frustrating. We have concluded that, with modifications, governments simply cannot control or determine the size of budgets—perhaps an almost radical conclusion. Three questions remain to be answered.

The first is this: Why cannot the "open-end commitments" which played such a big role in the rise in spending be abolished or at least modified?

There are somewhat different answers for different

programs; the reasons in the case of the farm program are not the same, for example, as the reasons in the case of veterans' pensions. But the generalization can be made that with flows of money this large an abolition of a program or a transfer of its financing to the states simply cannot be accomplished without serious disruptions and even injury. As we shall see in detail in the case of the farm program, disengagement is an almost impossibly painful problem.

The conservative regime did not think very seriously about the open-end commitments until it learned the dreary facts about what makes budgets go up. There were a few halfhearted proposals to change small items of expenditure from time to time, and, there were constant efforts to push Mr. Benson's solution to the farm problem. But not until 1959—the budget for fiscal year 1960—was there a really comprehensive effort to do something about the problem.

In that budget there were proposals to curb future increases in the veterans' pension program. There was an effort to raise statutory interest rates in several programs —rural electrification and college housing were the best examples—in order to force subsidized borrowers onto the private market, with guarantees instead of direct federal loans. There was an effort to reduce the federal share of the slum-clearance program, curb the program of aid to airports, transfer a few programs to the states. We shall have more to say on some of these items later.

But a few points about them are crucial in the present context.

Perhaps as important as anything is the fact that, even taken as a group, they were comparatively modest. While practically every one of them raised violent howls of opposition, the total expenditure effect—leaving out the possible long-run effect of the farm proposals—was, at best, to prevent future budgets from going up, not to reduce them. In the big programs, veterans and public assistance grants to the states, the conservative proposals seemed as if the mountain had labored and given birth to a mouse.

And then there is the painful truth that Congress paid no attention. The reason, I suggest, is the fact mentioned above—that when large money flows are involved, a cut-off or even a reduction produces genuine pain. A congressman from New York City does not have to be a "spendthrift" to oppose forcing his already pinched city to assume a larger share of slum clearance; his colleague from Indiana can scarcely vote to raise the electricity rates of his rural customers by changing the existing system. The truth of the matter is that there is a deep, and quite legitimate, self-interest in large groups of people in what exists, and no government can be expected to cut across that self-interest. The self-interest involved here is a totally different thing from the drive of "pressure groups" for new programs.

The next question can be disposed of quickly: What

of the allegation that the administration's troubles stemmed from having to deal most of the time with a Democratic Congress? The story of what went up in the budget contains most of the answer. The Democratic Congress did add the one-shot billion-dollar mortgage-buying program in 1958, and from time to time it raised the amounts involved in a few programs in the welfare field, such as medical research and old-age assistance. But the amounts were of small significance in relation to the total movement of the budget. Congress declined to enact the modest package of proposals for cutting down future budget commitments, but it is highly doubtful that this was because the Congress was Democratic. Finally, it was a Democratic Congress in 1957 that, after George Humphrey's explosion, put on perhaps the biggest "cut the budget" drive in history. It had almost no effect on the spending totals, of course, because Congress no longer has any real control over the budget, certainly not over the spending of a given year. It deals only with appropriations, not actual spending. Most spending is either related to national security—in which a year's outlays depend heavily on appropriations and decisions of prior years—or stems from laws on the books that Congress would not dream of repealing. In any case, even if what Congress did to appropriations mattered much, a "spendthrift Congress" problem was in no sense a major cause of the administration's frustration in its first six years. A few actions of Congress in 1958, chiefly in the highway field, may have a delayed upward effect on spending in 1960 and afterward, and it is possible that the more decisively liberal-Democratic Congress that took over in 1959 could have a more substantial effect on the budget totals in the future. But that has not been the trouble in the past, and the 1959 experience suggests doubt that it will be the trouble in the near future. The latest Congress has been hard put to raise spending, despite dark conservative fears after the 1958 election.

Finally, how about the idea, apparently so convincing to Mr. Humphrey, that "pressure groups" are the cause of bigger and bigger budgets. Well, I suppose the starving farmers of the 1930's who demanded price supports were a "pressure group," and so were the starving aged who demanded relief and now do not want to see it taken away. The air lines today, with their deplorably selfish opposition to accidents, are no doubt a pressure group too, and so are the motorists who feel that a car is designed to move and not to stand still in a perpetual traffic jam, and that greedy lot who like their mail delivered on time. The point, of course, is that practically every program the government spends *big* money on is either virtually essential or has origins in the past that make present changes almost impossible. True there are a few subsidies here and there (*very* few in our country, as distinct from some others) that might cause a raised eyebrow from the purist, some fairly frivolous river and harbor projects that clearly reflect local "pressure," a few defense establishments that would long since have been shut down but for the same kind of pressure. But all of this, in the big view, is peanuts. The problem is much greater than that.

Is there no hope then that the budget, if it cannot be reduced, can at least be held where it is? As we have noted, there appears a good chance of a small reduction in fiscal 1960, largely because of the expiration of several anti-recession programs, but the key point is that, at the very best, a new plateau of spending in the vicinity of $80 billion has now been reached. The answer to the question of whether the spending total can be held there, while the cold war lasts, has to be: Probably not. Defense, after all, still makes up half the budget, even though most of the increases recently have come on the civilian side. Hope might begin to dawn, outside of an end to the cold war, if the government could find a way of extricating itself from the farm and veterans' pension programs. But elsewhere—and probably in these areas too—the trend is going to be upward. Needless to say, there are large numbers of respectable people in the United States who feel emphatically that the trend *ought* to be upward, for both domestic and national security reasons. While it will undoubtedly remain essential in the fight against inflation to try to keep the budget under some sort of control, we ought to know from the conservative experience that we shall have to look elsewhere than to *lower* spending for our main weapons. This, if you will, is George Humphrey's lesson for posterity.

CHAPTER EIGHT

OF MONEY, TIGHT AND OTHERWISE

OF ALL THE MANEUVERINGS BY GOVERNMENTS IN THE financial field none is more mysterious than monetary policy. People can vaguely understand the importance of balanced budgets, but discount rates and "net borrowed reserves" rightly leave most citizens gasping in helpless confusion. And yet, with their unimpressive performance in fiscal policy (spending and taxing), the conservatives in power were almost forced to leave the main burden of fighting inflation to this weapon. The story is an instructive, though not yet conclusive, one.

At the outset of the story of money and its manipulation, one point must be cleared up. Monetary policy is the exclusive preserve of a complicated set of men and institutions called the Federal Reserve System, which by law, and since 1951 in practice, has been essentially "independent" of the government in power. This fact has real meaning. There have been occasions under both Mr. Truman and Mr. Eisenhower when the Federal Reserve System, the nation's central bank, took actions that were opposed by the President and his Secretary of the Treasury (invariably, I might add, actions of a "tightening" nature). But this independence, while real, was not a significant matter during most of the Eisenhower administration for the simple reason that the Federal Reserve System usually saw things the same way as the administration. Largely because of its basic structure, the Reserve System is strongly conservative. At some future time when a liberal Democrat again controls the White House the question of a fundamental clash of viewpoints and policies may again arise, as it arose in 1951 in a titanic struggle between the Federal Reserve and Mr. Truman from which the Federal Reserve emerged victorious. But during the years 1953–59 the Federal Reserve System was, in essence, an appendage of the conservatives in power. Despite the theory, and the fact, of independence, monetary policy under Eisenhower can be described and assessed as if it had been controlled by the President.

The Federal Reserve System had been created in 1913 not as a regulator of the economy nor as a knight for doing battle against inflation, but rather as an essentially technical scheme for avoiding the periodic "money panics" that had afflicted the United States economy. What has become its most important single instrument of policy—the buying and selling of government securities in the open market—was scarcely even envisaged by its creators. But over time the System first found itself required by events to take decisions and perform actions that had an effect on the economy as a whole, and, eventually, to become a major weapon of economic policy.

Essentially, the function of the Federal Reserve is to control the nation's money supply. Under all modern systems, omitting the intricacies of the process, private commercial banks generally create the money by expanding their loans and investments; but the fountainhead from which their money-creating power comes—the ultimate "printing press"—is the central bank. The central bank in the United States, the Federal Reserve System, sets limits to the money-creating capacity of the private banks by establishing a set of required "reserves" and then controlling the total amount of bank reserves that is available. It exercises this control through purchases and sales of government securities in the open market and by lending reserves to the banks at a variable "discount rate" of interest. A natural corollary to control of the total of bank reserves is a powerful influence over interest rates generally: when the demand for more loans in the society as a whole is high but the Federal Reserve is restricting the total lending and investing power of the banks, the price of money (interest rates) rises, and vice versa. The Federal Reserve does not fix interest rates, but influences them strongly by controlling one important element of the supply of lendable funds. Hence the national association of "tight money" with high interest rates, even though a major purpose of the "tight-money" policy is to curb the availability of credit rather than raise its cost.

Does all this have any real effect on real people, and hence on the real economy? That is one of the important open questions in current economic debate and one with which this chapter partly deals. In theory, controlling the lending power of the commercial banking system is a significant way of controlling total spending in the economy, and hence total demand. Spending can be reduced, assuming one wants to reduce it in order to curb an upward "pull" on prices, either by running a budget surplus or by "tight money." The latter is supposed to work by cutting the availability of credit. Obviously a man or a business who is turned away by his bank when he wants a loan has less money to spend. Curbing the money supply and curbing bank lending are two sides of the same coin—the coin of curbing total demand.

The idea of using the central bank's power over the money supply to stop inflation has been a matter of world-wide concern mainly in the 1950's. From the time of the establishment of the Federal Reserve System until World War II the typical problem of the economy was not inflation. After World War II, when there was such a problem, two serious deterrents existed to the use of this weapon. One was a nearly universal distrust of "classical" instruments of all kinds following the Great Depression, combined with an overwhelming fear, which flew in the face of the daily statistics, that the real problem would be another depression and not inflation. The second deterrent, more important in the United States, was the growth of the national debt. We need not at this point go into the details of the system to justify the generally agreed assertion that the very existence of this huge debt made resort to the use of "tight money" seem a highly risky business to the men in charge of the nation's finances under Mr. Truman. These fears turned out to be largely unfounded, but that did not make them any the less real and plausible.

In any case, nobody (with the interesting, and largely successful, exceptions of the Belgians, the Swiss, and the Germans) tried tight money until the 1950's. By that time it had finally dawned on even the most clever of the experts that the postwar economic problem was inflation, not depression. In the United States the great experiment began, as noted, after a struggle in 1951 between the central bank and the President. The Federal Reserve broke free and gradually began to apply its weapons of control whenever inflation was the problem, which was usually.

For a while it seemed that the rediscovery of tight money and higher interest rates as a regulator was something comparable to the discovery of the Holy Grail. As described in Chapter Five, prices in the United States began to stabilize very shortly after the Federal Reserve System resumed its freedom, and they remained stable for four years. The Federal Reserve had exercised its newly won freedom gently at first and then, as the economy showed signs of a typical boom after mid-1952, with increasing severity. Interest rates moved upward to levels unheard of for years—and prices remained stable. When the 1953–54 recession came along, the Federal Reserve quickly reversed policy toward "easy money," as it is classically supposed to do. But it appeared to have demonstrated that tight money, applied at times of boom, was capable of doing the job, even without any help from fiscal policy.

We all know now, of course, that in the next boom this illusion—an illusion, incidentally, that the Federal Reserve authorities themselves did not fully share—vanished. In the 1955–57 period the Federal Reserve pushed monetary restraint much further than in the previous boom. Interest rates rose higher (government bonds were selling at prices which meant an effective interest yield of 4 per cent, and by mid-1957 short-term interest rates, true to the classical pattern in times of monetary stringency, were as high as or higher than long-term rates). What is more, the money supply was held in check. Yet prices moved steadily upward.

Meanwhile, however, there was all manner of grumbling at what tight money allegedly *did* accomplish—namely, hurt small business, deter state and local government borrowing for such essential purposes as education, and slow down the construction of new housing. We shall return to these complaints in a moment. But meanwhile, what is the explanation for the failure of a seemingly vigorous, and certainly courageous, application of this weapon to halt the rise in the price level?

Leaving out altogether for present purposes the idea that it was a "new" inflation promoted by such things as the labor-union "cost push," and also leaving out the fact that fiscal policy was very little help, there appear to be three possible explanations. They are of considerable importance to our future.

The first emerges clearly from the financial statistics of the period. It will be recalled that the theory of tight money was that it would cut down on the power of the banking system to make loans, and thus cut down total spending. But from the beginning of 1955, when the first tentative moves toward restraint were made, until mid-1957, total bank loans actually rose by the enormous sum of $22 billion. In short, to perhaps 98 out of 100 desirous borrowers, *money was never really tight at all,* though it cost a bit more.

Why? The reason is somewhat complex and usually goes by the name of the "liquidity" of the banking system. The money supply, as we have noted, depends upon the total of bank loans *and investments*. Investments, in the main, mean bank holdings of government securities. During World War II the nation's banks had piled up an enormous hoard of government securities (this, in effect, was the "printing press" by which the war was largely financed). When the Federal Reserve began to clamp down on the total supply of new bank reserves, the banks merely had to sell these investments in order to get the funds to make loans. The sale of an investment, just like the repayment of a loan, has the technical effect of reducing the money supply, and the total money supply was kept from expanding much; but for practical inflation purposes, the real story is the expansion of loans. The nation's banking system was simply too "liquid"—supplied with enough ready-cash assets—to be fully and quickly responsive to an application of tight money. As we shall see, however, this may not always be true.

The second reason is related to the first, and is the subject of great and esoteric debate. It is the growth of the so-called "financial intermediaries"—savings banks, savings and loan associations, insurance companies, and pension funds—which can lend money but which are not in any direct sense controlled by Federal Reserve policy. This subject is much too technical for detailed exploration here. Suffice it to say that these newly expanded institutions cannot create money as the commercial banks can, but they do appear able to maintain a flow of lending even at times when the commercial banks are, at least theoretically, "tight." In classical monetary terms, their effect is to speed up the "velocity" or "turnover" of the existing money, and the result is an addition to the total flow of spending. To some degree, these institutions appear capable of blunting the tight-money weapon.

The third reason is the one commonly offered by the men in the Federal Reserve System itself. It is simply that they applied the tight-money policy too late and, at least at first, too softly. They will never admit that the world has so changed as to render monetary restraint ineffective (though neither will they claim that it can do the whole anti-inflation job by itself). In one official statement they (in this case, the presidents of the 12 Federal Reserve Banks) even claimed that they were tricked by the economic indicators in the period from late 1954 to mid-1955; they argued that the statistics, later revised, at the time "seriously understated" the pace and extent of the emerging boom, and that this in part accounted for their failure to move more rapidly with monetary restraint. We can note for future reference the fact that in the summer of 1958, as the next period of prosperity was getting under way after a slump, no such mistake was made. The Federal Re-

serve moved in the direction of restraint with unprece-
dented speed. If tight money fails to stop inflation again,
this excuse will no longer exist.

Neither, to the same extent as before, will the excuse
of bank "liquidity." Because of the response of the banking system to the 1955–57 tight-money period (in the
form of sales of government securities), and despite
some restoration of the hoard of investments during
the easy-money period accompanying the 1957–58 recession, the banks as a whole are less liquid now than
they have been at any time since the war: They have
fewer government securities that they can readily sell.
Next time, in theory at least, tight money should "bite"
harder and more quickly.

As for the "financial intermediaries" excuse, the
Federal Reserve people refuse to accept it as a serious
problem. Thus on every count, they can insist that tight
money as a regulator has yet to be fully tested. In
putting down still another item in the list of conservative
frustrations, it is perhaps well that we accept this contention and, as it were, give tight money another try.

Besides, even without these "excuses," it is highly
likely that the 1956–58 inflation would have been substantially worse but for the tight-money action of the
Federal Reserve. Certainly *some* borrowers failed to get
money and others decided they did not want to pay
the higher rates of interest. With the budget, to say
nothing of all the private forces in the economy, working

toward a higher price level, flooding the economy with new spending power through the device of cheap and easy money would certainly have increased total demand, and thus added to whatever forces were "pulling" prices up. Total demand can be excessive, even if there are no outright shortages of goods and services, by creating a climate in which sellers can easily cover higher costs by higher prices; in such a situation there are always, as it were, enough customers. Of course to the extent that the Federal Reserve *did* dam the total spending stream, it also probably curbed the rate of growth and investment, and probably of employment too. But that was the price it was designed to exact, on the assumption that a more rapid advance of the economy would have made the concurrent inflation and the ensuing slump worse.

What of the complaint that tight money, besides slowing growth, works severe hardship on just those sectors of the economy that can stand it least? The idea is that big business can always get the money it needs but that the pinch acts on small business, state and local government, and hardest of all, on housing (through the effect on the availability of mortgage money). My own belief is that there is less here than meets the eye. The statistics on loans to small business are, as with most statistics, susceptible of differing interpretations, and they are rather inadequate to boot. But what they do appear to show is that there has been no serious curtailment of ordinary short-term, bank-type credit to the small as opposed to the big. One very good reason, of course, is that *nobody's* credit has been very seriously curtailed during recent experiments with tight money; another is that thousands of banks can, in effect, lend *only* to small businesses because they are small themselves, and these banks, under the workings of our system, have been on the whole the ones least pinched by the reserve shortage imposed by the Federal Reserve. As for state and local governments, some bond issues were undoubtedly canceled or postponed, often because of arbitrary and quite foolish legal ceilings on interest rates that could be paid. But it is also a fact that the total of these bond issues was reaching new records during the period in question, and that the curtailment was really not very serious. The one sector that does seem to be hurt is housing, and this is something of an irony. For it is housing, above all, that is financed by the new "financial intermediaries." In their commercial banking function, the banks make few mortgage loans. If this indicates that the Federal Reserve System is right in its contention that the intermediaries are not a very serious obstacle to the efficacy of tight money, so much the better. Mortgage money *did* dry up when money was tight. In any case, the stringency of mortgage credit almost certainly slowed down housing starts, beginning in about mid-1956. To keep this matter in perspective, however, there was never anything like a collapse in housing—as was so constantly predicted by some spokesmen for the industry—and the American people are not afflicted by such a housing shortage that a slowdown in new starts constitutes a major hardship.

In sum, tight money did not do the job for the conservatives when the chips were down (though it certainly kept the inflation from being worse), and it was criticized while trying. But if we have to reach an essentially gloomy conclusion about future possibilities of fighting inflation with lower budgets, the verdict on tight money must still be the Scottish one of "not proved." It should not be many more years before we will know the answer one way or the other.

CHAPTER NINE

CARE AND FEEDING OF THE NATIONAL DEBT

IF THE CONSERVATIVES DESCENDING ON WASHINGTON
in early 1953 were distressed at the budget picture they
found, their dismay was no less over the state of the
national debt. For a while at least, as we have seen,
they appeared to get the budget picture under control.
But a solution of the debt problem has remained elusive
throughout their term, and may well do so indefinitely.
The list of conservative frustrations must include this
item, too, though to their credit the conservatives in
this case, as distinct from that of the budget, had relatively few illusions to begin with.

What is the "problem" of the national debt? The first

point to make is that the problem is *not* the $285 billion size of the debt as such, huge though that sum is. George Humphrey occasionally let slip the thought that, in his view, the debt would have to be reduced in order to strengthen the "credit" of the government. His fears were peculiar to himself. Few people, conservative or liberal, doubt that the government can always borrow more money if necessary. What is more, the economy has, as it were, "grown up to" the present debt and has learned to live fairly comfortably with it. There is an absolute need in the ordinary course of financial business for a very large supply of government securities to be outstanding, and a radical reduction of the debt (if that were possible, which it is not) would cause considerable upset.

But if there is nothing inherently harmful about the over-all size of the debt, its structure and ownership are another matter. For reasons which we shall note in a moment, the debt has to be *managed*. Between five and ten times a year the men in the Treasury must make major decisions relating to the debt. In making them, they have certain objectives in mind and are aware of certain practical obstacles to achieving those objectives. The story of debt management under the conservatives is, on the whole, the story of the triumph of the obstacles over the objectives.

The debt has to be managed mainly because a substantial part of it reaches maturity each year and must be paid off or replaced with new debt. Leaving out the approximately $25 billion in three-month Treasury bills which "roll over" almost automatically, leaving out the constant maturing of savings bonds, and leaving out the portion of the debt held by the Federal Reserve System, a little over $20 billion has been maturing each year. Furthermore, under our present tax system, even when the budget is balanced the Treasury must raise new cash at least once or twice during any year. This is because tax receipts tend to be bunched in the first six months of the calendar year, meaning that the government must undertake at least temporary borrowing in the last six months. If there is a budget deficit besides, of course, this new cash borrowing operation is all the greater.

The way these refunding and new borrowing operations are carried out has effects on the economy which are complex and not fully understood, but which can be summed up this way: The wrong kind of debt management makes the problem of controlling inflation by the other weapons—chiefly monetary policy—much tougher. There is, in short, an anti-inflationary way to manage the debt and a relatively inflationary way. The frustration of the conservatives was that, for reasons beyond their control, they frequently had to use the inflationary way.

In brief, the anti-inflationary way to manage the national debt is to "fund" it—shift as much of it as possible into securities of relatively long term and out of securities maturing in one or two years or even less. If there is, say, a maturity of $7 billion in a given month and the Treasury replaces the entire maturing issue with a one-year certificate, then no progress has been made toward a less inflationary debt structure; if, on the other hand, it is able to replace the maturing securities with, say, $1 billion in thirty-year bonds and $2 billion in seven-year bonds and only $4 billion in one-year certificates, it has made very important progress.

There are two chief reasons for this. The first relates to the frequency and size of debt-management operations. The longer the maturity structure of the debt, the fewer—or the smaller, which is just as important— are the maturities in each year. Today's thirty-year bond can be forgotten until 1990. When the Treasury goes to the market, the Federal Reserve System must usually modify its monetary policy, at least temporarily, in order to help the Treasury out. In short, the Federal Reserve could operate much better if the Treasury had to refinance only, say, $10 billion a year instead of more than $20 billion.

The second relates to the general "liquidity" of the economy. A short-term government security is near-money; no matter who holds it, it can be readily converted into cash, which then can be spent or loaned. A longer-term instrument is usually a repository of genuine savings, where the holder does not want immediate cash; in any case, by nature the longer-term instrument fluctuates much more sharply in price than a short-term instrument (unless it is a savings bond), and thus imposes a penalty on the holder who wants to sell it for cash when bond prices are low—that is, the times of tight money and high interest rates when the Federal Reserve is trying to curb spending. It is often said that excessive short-term debt has the added disadvantage of adding to the money supply because banks buy short-term securities, and bank purchases amount to the creation of new money. Recent experience casts some doubt on this idea; corporations and other holders of funds available for short-term investment have been the big buyers of Treasury bills. Bank holdings appear to depend more on Federal Reserve actions than on debt management policy, at least so long as other buyers of these securities exist. At some point the banks might be the last resort—a genuine fear of the authorities in 1959 —but meanwhile the "liquidity" case alone is enough to make the battler against inflation seek to stretch out the maturities of the debt as much and as often as possible.

When the Republicans took office they found what was in their view a deplorable debt structure. A lot of long-term issues had been sold during World War II, but since the war there had been almost no funding operations by the Truman administration. Thus each month that passed brought the average maturity of the entire outstanding debt a month closer, and each year the Treasury had to handle more financing operations.

The conservative frustration is revealed in a single figure. When they took office, the average time to maturity of the debt was 5 years and 3 months. Six years later it was 4 years and 9 months—if anything a shade worse than they had found it. The size and frequency of the annual financing operations was as bad as ever (even President Eisenhower complained about this arcane problem at a late 1958 press conference). The outstanding amount of Treasury bills—the shortest-term securities—had risen by mid-1959 to a record high, and the liquidity in the economy stemming from the national debt was probably greater than ever.

Why this failure to achieve a major objective? Common sense supplies the major part of the answer, and the conservatives knew this all along: Every month that passes shortens the average maturity of the debt by a month. The Treasury, as Undersecretary Randolph Burgess never tired of pointing out, has to run fast to stand still. It can legitimately be argued that it was a considerable accomplishment for the Republicans to have prevented the average maturity schedule from shortening much over the six years, as it had previously been shortening year by year since the end of World War II. The Eisenhower Treasury in the six years floated the first truly long-term bonds (twenty years or more) since the war, $7 billion worth in the first six years, and it was occasionally able to sell securities in the five-to-ten-year range. This was at least a change in direction, and an accomplishment of considerable proportions.

But the story does not end there. Why could the conservatives not do better? Once again, the real world proved tougher than the theoretical world.

The first major financial decision of the new administration came only a few months after it took office when George Humphrey and Randolph Burgess took the bit in their teeth and floated the first long-term marketable government bond since the war. To make it sell, they put on it a 3¼ per cent interest coupon—also the highest since the war—to the outraged, if somewhat confused, cries of the Democrats in Congress. But alas, shortly thereafter the government bond market collapsed in near panic and Mr. Humphrey's proud new bond slunk shamefacedly below par. The buyers were unhappy, the Democrats were unhappy, and Mr. Humphrey, who had learned his first lesson in debt management, was unhappiest of all. The bonds soon became known as the "Humphrey-Dumphries."

The lesson from this experience was to strike home with equal force in late 1956 and early 1957. It is this: When the economy is booming, when savings are being employed as fast as they are generated, and when the Federal Reserve is applying monetary restraint, it is just about impossible in the present American system to sell long-term government bonds without causing such disruption that the disadvantages outweigh the advantages. This is so even though such times are precisely those when, according to traditional theory, sale of long-term bonds is desirable to lessen liquidity, slow down private investment, and curb activity generally.

But then why not float them aggressively when the economy is in a slump and the Federal Reserve's policy is one of ease? The answer is that that is the very time when the government wants more spending, more liquidity, more investment. In the 1957–58 recession Secretary Anderson did float several long bonds—an act of considerable courage. But he dared not be too headstrong about it.

It has turned out that there is *never* a good time for funding the debt in the really massive amounts that would be necessary to get the debt structure into sound shape. The best times have seemed to be when slumps were just beginning or when they were just ending. But even the latter did not work during the recovery from the 1957–58 slump. One reason, ironically, was that the Federal Reserve, as noted in the last chapter, moved much more quickly in the direction of restraint once the recovery had begun. This was no doubt proper, and certainly courageous; but partly as a result of this switch the money markets changed direction with equal speed, bond prices collapsed, things were upset for months, and the Treasury had no choice but to confine itself to offerings of short-term securities. The amount of very short-term debt rose to record levels; the Treasury managed to raise the money to cover the $12.5 billion deficit only by adding still further to the economy's liquidity, thus raising fears of potentially inflationary spending power during the ensuing period of prosperity.

The basic dilemma was described briefly at the end of Chapter Five: "Tight money sometimes makes anti-inflationary debt management more difficult, yet 'inflationary' debt management makes tight money more difficult to carry out." The dilemma should not be over-rated, but the conservatives discovered its reality as decisions came up from month to month. My hunch is that debt management, while important, is less so than fiscal or monetary policy in the anti-inflation arsenal. One hopes so. For a courageous conservative Treasury found it could not run nearly as fast as it wanted to—and it stood still, or even fell back a little.

CHAPTER TEN

A FINAL THOUGHT ON INFLATION

A SOPHISTICATED AMERICAN WHO IS PERSUADED that creeping inflation—say a 25 to 30 per cent rise in prices in ten years—is to be the normal condition of the economy can make an impressive case. As he picks up the telephone to his broker to put still more of his money in the stock market, he might argue something like this:

"The experts are not agreed on the question of whether new forces in our economy, chiefly labor unions and perpetual high employment, are exerting a significant upward thrust upon prices that did not exist until very recently, or whether inflation results from the same old things—too much total spending, too much money supply. But it does not really matter which side is right. For it looks to me as if the 'old' forces will be quite sufficient to cause rising prices in America, even if the new ones are not important, as I believe they are. My evidence is what has happened under a conservative government—bigger budgets than ever before, big deficits at the slightest sign of slump, caution and seeming impotence in monetary policy, a huge short-term debt that seems to get bigger rather than smaller. In short, while I feel sure the 'cost push' will continue to work, I do not need it to convince myself that prices are going to go on rising. Hello? Sell those 3½'s of 1990 and pick up another hundred shares of DuPont."

The analysis is clever and persuasive. But it overlooks one potentially important point—a point at the heart of perhaps the greatest unresolved question of all. The issue is this: Can prices go on climbing upward by 2 or 3 per cent a year indefinitely without causing severe trouble, including trouble to the prices of stocks on the Stock Exchange?

The Federal Reserve Board, and conservatives generally, say they cannot. A condition of creeping inflation, so this position goes, gradually changes the way the economy operates. Businesses tend to build excessive inventories to beat price increases. Equally important, they build new plant capacity earlier rather than later, even if it is not needed immediately, because it will just cost more to wait. Consumers tend to spend a bit more, save a bit less. Investors, seeking a hedge against inflation, run up prices of stocks and a few other things to "speculative" levels. Because this whole system is essentially artificial, it must collapse into slump in the economy, unemployment, lower profits, and a sharply lower stock market. The very act of betting on continuation of inflation brings the collapse about all the sooner. And we have yet to see in the postwar period the really bad slumps that can result from this sort of condition.

All of this is, up to now, mostly theoretical. We have never lived before with a widespread belief in the concept of indefinite slow inflation, and no one really knows what a popular conviction that inflation is inevitable will do. For example, contrary to what might be thought, there is some indication that people with such a conviction actually buy more life insurance rather than less, on the ground that more will be needed when the time comes to collect. Thus savings grow even though inflation "erodes" savings such as life insurance. There is no sure evidence yet that business decisions will in fact be drastically changed by the conviction that *slow* inflation is likely to be a continuing condition. Furthermore, who is to say when a slump comes that it was the inevitable aftermath of a preceding slow inflation, especially when the conservatives have told us all along that "ups and downs" in the economy are inevitable? And finally, the gambler on inflation can take some comfort in the belief that when slumps do come, the government is likely to take inflationary, and successful, measures to cure them—bigger spending, bigger deficits, easy money.

In short, the theory of the conservatives that creeping inflation, and the belief in creeping inflation, will inevitably bring a correction much more painful than anything we have experienced thus far in the postwar period, is far from self-evident. It may not even be true. But then again it might be; and if it is, a lot of losses will be suffered in the process of finding out. Among the losers, presumably, will be our investor who sold his bonds and bought DuPont.

The Federal Reserve and the conservative administration do not want to test their theory. They would prefer to stop the inflation for once and all. But can they in present conditions—cold war, open-end budget commitments, an ornery national debt, a liquid banking system—do anything to stop the rise in prices before the feared boom-bust cycle occurs? Can they effectively tackle inflation by the classic methods, even assuming the classic methods can work in the day of big labor and big business?

The story of the conservatives in power indicates that they cannot. But it is not yet a complete story. I suggest that what can be concluded from the years of conservative government is not that the old methods do not work, nor even that they cannot be effectively applied in modern conditions, but simply that the job of applying them is much more difficult than anyone had previously supposed.

I have noted earlier a hesitant conclusion that the forces of the "new" inflation indeed exist—that the "cost push" is a real force to be reckoned with—but that the heart of the inflation problem is still demand. That is, if demand is kept in bounds by classic government financial weapons, the inflation will be very slight—say 1 per cent a year instead of the far more serious 2 or 3 per cent. There is some preliminary evidence in Britain that this conclusion may be correct.

An equally important conclusion is the one suggested above—that use of the classic weapons is not impossible but only more difficult than we had supposed. The budget clearly is not fully controllable, but it appears likely that the rate of increase can be kept under some sort of check. Monetary policy has obvious limits, but conditions for its success may be better now than at any time in the postwar period. Aggressive funding of the debt in small amounts at every propitious moment might at least keep that problem from getting any worse. In short, this and future conservative governments are just going to have to be even tougher—at the cost, incidentally, of failing to provide some government services that would be desirable, a slower rate of construction of housing than many people would like, possibly a slower than "optimum" rate of economic growth, even higher unemployment than we have been used to. All of these things are reasonably likely results from *effective* efforts to check demand. Nothing in the conservative philosophy, performance, or courage suggests that future conservative governments would be unwilling to pay this price to achieve the goal of reasonable prosperity without inflation, plus, as they see it, probably less frequently interrupted prosperity to boot. As the sixth year of the conservatives in power ended, inflation had once again been followed, and temporarily stopped, by a slump. One comforting thought as the forces of inflation are gathering for the next onslaught on the price level is that from now on conservative governments will know better what they are up against.

PART TWO

Finance and the battle against inflation are at the heart of a conservative view of government. But to tell the story of the Eisenhower regime's performance in that area is by no means to complete the story of conservatives in power.

We have suggested in Chapter Two that a conservative portrait includes other elements. And even if it did not, the economic policy of government inevitably covers more matters than the budget, monetary policy, and debt management.

In the succeeding chapters, we shall look into those other matters, item by item. They do not have *the close interconnections of the elements of financial policy but stand, as it were, on their own. Many of them do, however, reflect back on the basic subject of finance and cannot be considered apart from the foregoing, first part of this book.*

Do they too tell a story of frustration? The record differs from item to time, but the basic pattern is scarcely one of crowning success in achieving conservative objectives. An apparent exception may be a good place to begin.

CHAPTER ELEVEN

A TALE OF TWO SLUMPS

IT IS OFTEN SAID THAT THE YOUNGER GENERATION IN the United States shows an almost brutal unawareness of the awful days of the Great Depression of the 1930's. But it would be difficult to persuade a Republican politician that *anyone* in the United States has forgotten those days. For the conservative frustration in perhaps the most important aspect of economic policy of them all—maintaining prosperity and halting recessions if they come—has been political, not economic. The conservatives, or something, halted the two slumps that afflicted the economy during the first six years of the regime, and yet the election immediately following each slump produced sharp Democratic gains in Congress. This was particularly true after the 1957–58 recession, when the Democratic majority in Congress rose to levels not seen since the 1930's; the big Democratic victory occurred in an election in which it was fairly generally agreed that the only issue of any great importance was the economic one.

This political result does not, however, negate what seems, by the usual test of results, a highly successful conservative performance in business-cycle policy. It is difficult to have slumps much briefer or milder than those of 1953–54 and 1957–58. Whether conscious action by the government in power was the reason for this mildness and brevity is the main question examined by this chapter, and the answer holds some interesting lessons for the future. But meanwhile, it is worth taking a closer look at the type of thinking about slumps that the conservatives brought with them to Washington.

Are present-day Republicans Keynesian? That is, do they believe that declines in economic activity are likely to become severe and prolonged unless the government does something about them, and that therefore government action—action involving large deficits in the budget—is a prerequisite for cure? This question cannot be answered with a flat "yes." The main reason is that some of the Republicans who came to Washington in 1953 were and are far more Keynesian than others.

George Humphrey remains convinced to this day that big government deficits—caused by new spending programs or tax cuts or both—probably do more harm than good in the cure of slumps. His theory, almost unanimously rejected by the economic profession, is that big deficits will so undermine business confidence that business spending will be cut by far more than government spending (or personal spending made possible by tax cuts) will rise. It would appear that his theory had been dealt a rather harsh blow by the performance of the economy during and after the 1957–58 slump, when the deficit reached record proportions and business spending actually increased, sooner than anyone had thought likely. But still, there the theory is.

From Humphrey on one side opinions range through various shades to men like Arthur Burns on the other. Burns not only did not fear deficits. He believed in both the efficacy and necessity of government action, on a massive scale if conditions called for it. Is there, then, no common ground among the conservatives in this crucial matter?

I believe there has proved to be less common ground here than on any other major point of policy, and that this fact, as we shall see, suggests some disturbing possibilities for the future. But there are some elements of the question on which the conservatives do agree.

The most important, touched upon briefly in Chapter Two, is a belief that slumps are probably inevitable in a free economy, and thus that periodic unemployment cannot be prevented. Slumps come about because of more or less inevitable excesses that accompany booms— chiefly excesses in the building of inventories and, usually, excesses in the building of plant and equipment. If the period of prosperity has included substantial inflation, these excesses, as we have seen, are likely, according to conservative thinking, to be all the greater.

This point about the inevitability of slumps may seem self-evident to many of us, but it is still a distinguishing character of conservative thought. Many liberals would never admit the inevitability of slumps. They appear persuaded that proper government policies to pump up demand can in fact make the gross national product higher in every quarter than in the quarter before—and if this means a little more inflation, so be it.

A second common feature of conservative thought about the business cycle is a conviction that slumps should not be "over-cured." That is, government spending and tax-reducing and monetary easing actions should be only sufficient to do the job, for if they are more than sufficient the slump is likely to give way to renewed inflation. Deficient total demand would quickly turn into excessive total demand, with the likelihood of another and worse slump to follow the resulting inflation.

It might be said of the extreme view represented by Humphrey, of course, that this school does not believe recessions should be "cured" by government action at all.

Finally, the conservatives tend to have considerable faith in the recuperative powers of the private economy in all normal circumstances. In this it might be said that they are positively anti-Keynesian. They do not believe, as Keynes did, that a modern industrial economy has a built-in tendency to sink into prolonged depression. Rather they think its "norm" is expansion and that slumps are normally in the nature of brief corrections. They have plenty of ancient and modern evidence for this view.

So much for the business-cycle philosophy of the men who were confronted with the two recessions. I feel that the difference over the question of deficits is more important than the several similarities. What, then, happened when in fact the economy showed some indigestion and started twice on the lugubrious downward slope?

There is a pattern about recessions. The economy has been rolling along prosperously. Business has been gradually building inventories and new plant. Then some "external" force acts to cut down demand in one or more major sectors. Very soon both existing inventories and existing plant appear excessive. Even a relatively small change in final demand can cause a reversal from inventory accumulation to inventory liquidation. Businesses which are using up inventories are not placing orders, thus some other businesses are not producing. Soon the change in the inventory sector becomes much the biggest downward force in total demand. Layoffs begin, personal incomes are reduced, and, eventually, consumer spending—the major sector of total demand —begins falling. Meanwhile, investment in additional plant and equipment is also falling, with a consequence of still more layoffs, as existing capacity seems more than adequate. If all this goes on long enough—and it does not take much more than a year—obviously the initial dip can turn into a downward spiral of severe proportions. As an aside, I report what I believe to be the majority view among economists that there is nothing automatic about our modern economy that makes such a spiral (i.e., a severe depression) impossible, though the economy is far less vulnerable than it once was, as we shall see.

The story of the start of slumps, then, is the story of where and why some element of final demand fell off—either some purely external factor or, possibly, the automatic reaction to a previous excess of demand in one or more sectors of the economy. The story of how slumps are cured is the story of how the aggregate of final demand was maintained long enough for the inventory cycle to run its course and expansion to resume again.

The account of where demand fell off to start the two slumps of the 1950's must begin with a question. Did the conservative government *cause* the slumps by its previous anti-inflation policy, chiefly the tight-money policy? The conservatives argue, of course, that not only did their anti-inflation efforts not cause the slumps but, by moderating the prior booms to some extent, they helped assure that the slumps would be brief and mild. For example, the Federal Reserve Board is convinced that inventory excesses in both early 1953 and early 1957 were less than they otherwise would have been because of the preceding monetary restraint (accumulating inventory requires borrowing, and presumably there was some deterrent in the form of higher interest rates, if not in an actual shortage of credit). From the liberals comes the opposite claim that the credit squeeze slowed down housing activity, thus curbing an important sector of final demand, and eventually worked to reduce business investment in plant and equipment and construction generally, thus hitting hard at other key sectors: in short, that tight money played a major role in bringing on the slump.

I do not know the answer in this dispute, but my hunch is that in the actual world of the 1950's the government's prior tight-money policies did not make much difference in either direction. A *budget* action, as we shall see, had something to do with the 1957–58 slump, but I doubt that monetary restraint either brought on the slumps, or, by sufficiently curbing the prior inflation, played a big role in keeping the slumps mild. I am even more convinced of the former than of the latter. It is difficult indeed to make much of a case that the conservatives "brought on" either slump, certainly not purposely and almost certainly not as a consequence of their previous efforts to moderate the boom. The reason is that the main causes of each slump were quite obvious, at least in hindsight, and unrelated to tight money.

The single important cause of the 1953–54 slump was the end of the Korean War and a consequent very sharp reduction in government spending on defense. Expenditures for national security, at seasonally adjusted annual rates, fell steadily from \$53.2 billion in the second quarter of 1953 until bottom was reached at \$40.5 billion in the fourth quarter of 1954. This was a major reduction in final demand. The usual inventory consequences followed, and then the typical decline in business fixed investment.

The causes of the 1957–58 slump were a little more numerous. One was a big drop in exports, which had been artificially inflated by the Suez crisis and a few other factors. Another was a virtual cutoff in defense orders starting in about July of 1957, caused by a fear that defense spending was running so high as to produce a deficit and thus require more Treasury borrowing than the national debt limit allowed. (What an irony this was! The resulting slump brought a huge deficit and the debt limit had to be raised by far more than anything a slightly higher rate of defense spending could have required.) This, incidentally, is our example of a conservative action that *did* help bring on a slump—an action whose roots were the desire to curb inflation by curbing spending. Defense orders fell off far more rapidly than actual spending, but the shift in orders alone had important consequences for inventories and confidence. The third cause was a decline in plant and equipment spending. This had been going through a major boom that eventually just petered out, almost certainly more from a quite natural satiation of desire for more capacity than from the restraint on new borrowing imposed by tight money. Finally a bad year for automobiles certainly did not help any, though I believe this was more a result of the slump than a cause. It might be argued that the sluggishness in housing that began in the latter half of 1956 also contributed to the start of the slump, and that tight money was partly responsible; but housing, while not strong, was not *declining* much and cannot be charged with actually reducing final demand significantly in the last half of 1957, when the slump began.

We have seen that the cure of slumps is found in those events and measures that add to or maintain the aggregate of final demand so as to allow the inventory liquidation cycle to proceed for its necessarily limited time span and then reverse itself. The story of what maintained final demand in the two slumps of the 1950's is the real story of conservative business-cycle policy, and it is a revealing one.

One thing that maintained demand, it should be said at the outset, is the very nature of our modern economy, quite apart from any actions of the government. Because of the gradual shift of our labor force and other resources out of the volatile manufacturing and mining and farming industries into trade, government, finance, and services, it is quite probable that the economy has, as it were, made itself more slump-resistant. Whole sectors of the economy do not feel slumps, at least for a long time, and confidence is therefore less easy to shatter. In effect, a higher proportion of jobs are, by their nature, secure. Less than one-fifth of all workers are now employed in production jobs in factories, for example. Our system of wage setting, if it poses problems during the upward part of the cycle, probably acts as a significant check on the downswing; it is clear, in any case, that wages as a whole kept rising through all three slumps with an inevitable, and important, effect on the total of personal incomes and hence on consumer spending. This is not as much of a blessing as it seems, for higher wages mean either reduced profits or higher prices, thus subtracting from other incomes. But it seems fairly clear that wage rigidity on the downside helps prevent the cumulative spiral from getting under way.

Still, the economy is not immune from the spiral because of all this. Almost inevitably, the margin of demand that must be supplied to halt the downward movement and start the upswing has to come from government. That has certainly been the case in the three postwar slumps.

The story of the government's role in our two slumps, then, begins with the fact that demand was partly maintained by the famous "built-in stabilizers," which required no conscious act of policy at all. The most important of these is of course unemployment compensation. In both slumps it worked like clockwork, making up about one-third of the loss of wages resulting from layoffs. This is a device, pure and simple, for automatic expansion of government spending. Presumably because it is financed outside the regular budget and adds only to the more significant "cash" deficit, even Mr. Humphrey does not seem to object to it. Another is farm price supports, which operate in booms or slumps to maintain income of an important portion of the farm population (though of course supports have enormous drawbacks, too). A third is the whole structure of payments for the aged, both those who collect social security on retirement and those who are poor and collect relief under the system of public assistance partly financed from Washington. These payments tend, if anything, to expand in slumps. Finally, the workings of our corporate tax system help to create conditions under which dividends can be maintained, at least for the first year of a slump; the drop in profits is 50 per cent absorbed by the government. All of these "automatic" items put together are not enough by themselves, however, to guarantee that the downward spiral can never take hold. More is required.

One "extra" that occurred in both slumps was help, and probably valuable help, from a switch by the Federal Reserve System to easy money. Aided by certain modifications in down payments under government-backed mortgage programs, and similar devices, easy money undoubtedly made its mark in the housing field by loosening mortgage credit. A veritable boom in housing helped the economy out of both slumps, and out of the 1948–49 recession as well. The switch to easy money presumably allowed at least a few other borrowers, who had been deterred under tight money, to get money and spend it, but this is difficult to prove. The total of bank loans declined with the general economy in each slump, and the old analogy of easy money in a time of slump being like "pushing on a string" still has some merit. You cannot force people to borrow and spend simply by making credit available. In the 1957–58 recession the switch to easy money did, however, clearly open the way to a flood of state and local government borrowing, some of which apparently had been held back during the preceding period of high interest rates. Finally, easy money has the effect of making banks buyers, rather than sellers, of government securities and other investments, thus pushing up market prices; this in turn adds to the liquidity and spending power of those who hold these securities. Bank investments expanded by over $10 billion in the first six months of 1958, and some of this new money must have found its way into the spending stream (the increase in bank investments was so great, indeed, as to raise fears of an "over-cure" of the slump and thus of subsequent inflation through immediate and later effects on the money supply). It seems quite clear that easy money is effective as a slump remedy in proportion as the policy has been tight before, and that its greatest effect is in the early stages of a slump before the downward spiral takes hold. It is also clear that this is now, in practical terms, almost as much an "automatic" stabilizer as the other, more familiar, ones. Certainly governments will use it every time, without difficulty and without complaint.

Still another item in the automatic—or nearly automatic—list of stabilizers is state and local government spending, quite apart from any stimulus to this spending from lower interest rates. We know, as a fact, that state-local spending has been rising by about $3 billion a year for a decade, whether the general economy was in slump or boom. Here, it appears, is the real fruit of population growth. In the purely private sector of the economy, as any family knows, another child does not add a dollar to spending power; if it did, India would be the most prosperous nation on earth. But a rising population does create more *public* spending, almost entirely on a state-local level. We have been able to count on added demand from this source in every postwar slump, and it is a fair guess that we can continue to do so.

Note that all of these items are *government* devices for increasing or maintaining total demand in the economy, as an offset to the tendency of private demand to spiral downward. Most of them involve government spending. They are, in effect, Keynesian, without conservatives having to admit that they are. And a case can be made that put together these items are enough by themselves to make the economy slump-resistant.

But, as I have suggested before, it is likely that even this impressive array of devices and changes is not a sufficient guarantee against the downward spiral. The forces that can drive the economy downward are of impressive magnitude, and possibly greater today in a bigger economy than they were when severe slumps were fairly common. And so that brings us to the other actions of the government to augment demand, conscious or otherwise, that made what was probably the crucial difference in the two slumps of the 1950's. The story they tell is far more one of luck than of management.

In the 1953–54 recession there was only one that counted, but it was a whopper. It was a series of tax cuts totaling about $7.4 billion. But these tax cuts—certainly in the mind of the man who counted most, George Humphrey—were not undertaken to cure the slump.

There were four items in the package. The most important were the first two—a $3 billion cut in personal income taxes and $2 billion from the abolition of the corporate excess profits tax. Both were due to happen under existing law on January 1, 1954.

Now Arthur Burns, the administration's chief economist at the time, was delighted at this fortunate coincidence. He has since made quite a point of the fact that as early as September, 1953, Secretary Humphrey in a speech gave assurances that these tax reductions would take place on schedule and that no effort would be made to extend the existing rates, even though the budget was still in deficit. This, to Burns, was an example of anti-recession "policy."

But Humphrey saw the picture quite differently. First he saw the fact that it would be a practical and political impossibility to have the law changed; it would have required a special session of Congress. Second, he knew that spending, with the end of the

Korean War, was heading downward and that these tax reductions could be made without *increasing* the already rather modest budget deficit. He always called these tax reductions a sort of payment in advance for spending reductions that were already in the cards. He never dreamed of them as a Keynesian remedy for a slump.

Thus if the law had not by chance been written the way it was, and if spending had not been on what was, for anti-recession purposes, an unfortunate downward trend, there is no assurance that this big tax cut would ever have been made. By the same token, there is no assurance that the 1953–54 slump would have been cured so easily.

The other two tax cuts were $1 billion in excises pushed through by Congress over the initial *objections* of Mr. Humphrey, and the big $1.4 billion tax reform and revision bill. We shall take up the latter in a later chapter. For the moment, suffice it to say that it was of such a nature that it could have almost no impact on the immediate problem of the slump; among other things, it did not clear Congress until the slump had already hit bottom.

In the 1957–58 recession there was no single action quite as outstanding as the tax cuts of the earlier slump. But again it turns out that the ones that mattered most were not taken consciously for anti-slump reasons.

The most important was probably the sharp reversal

of the defense order situation. The Russian sputniks of October, 1957, were far more important than the slump in achieving this most desirable result. In any case orders, which had fallen to $7 billion in the last six months of 1957, rose to $13 billion in the first six months of 1958. Orders went through far more severe gyrations than actual spending, on both the downside and the upside. But it appears probable that it is orders, rather than spending, that have the main "secondary" effects on inventories and even employment.

Then there was a surprisingly large jump in the gamut of social security payments, quite apart from the usual increase associated with slumps. Various amendments to the law enacted in the three previous years had brought in farmers, women between 62 and 65 years of age, and the disabled. Payments under all these programs began to swell at about the same—and most auspicious—time, the winter of 1957–58. They added about $1.2 billion to the annual rate of personal incomes. The big highway program, enacted long before the slump, was gathering steam as the slump began. Finally, a federal employees' pay raise had long been overdue because of past inflation, and its enactment added the tidy sum of $1.4 billion to the spending stream at annual rates, plus a lump-sum retroactive payment of $400 million. The last-named took effect after the bottom had been reached, but it did its bit in producing what turned out to be the sharpest of the three postwar recoveries (on the charts the 1957–58–59 period was a V rather than the more typical saucer).

True, there were some conscious government moves as well. The usual housing devices were employed, augmented this time by $1 billion in special mortgage purchase funds pushed through by the Democratic Congress *over the President's objections*—almost surely the most important single action adopted for specifically anti-recession reasons. We have already noted that housing, helped also by easy money, took a sharp upturn in the spring of 1958. There was an emergency unemployment compensation program to extend benefits for those who had exhausted them under regular state laws, worth about $400 million. The highway program was given a boost by a special anti-recession bill, though the main effects of the bill could not be felt until the slump was long over; it, too, was a far bigger program than the President had asked for. A flood of directives went out in an effort to speed up various public works, without increasing their total magnitude, but it is doubtful if more than $200 million was added to the total spending stream by this. Taken together, these measures came to considerably less in amount and impact than those—mainly the reversal in defense orders—which occurred for reasons unconnected with the recession. Indeed, the only significant spending measure backed by the administration was the emergency jobless pay bill, and by all odds the most important single decision the administration took was the decision—correct as it turned out—to *oppose* a tax cut.

Needless to say, all of this—helped also by a fortuitous spurt in farm income—added up to a cure, bolstering demand in various sectors of the economy. The total rise in government outlays was impressive—greater than the raw figures imply. Because spending for defense (as distinct from orders) was actually declining during the crucial six months from October, 1957, through March, 1958, the impact of the rise in government outlays is disguised in the totals. Furthermore, such items as the increase in defense orders, the spurt in highway contracts under the already existing program, and the mortgage-purchase commitments under the special anti-recession housing bill had an economic impact well in advance of the disbursement of money from the Treasury. Finally, the array of actions, mostly not taken for anti-recession reasons, that drastically increased the total of federal spending in fiscal year 1959, even if some took hold after the economy had already made its turn, added greatly to the rapidity of the recovery. Total cash payments to the public rose from $80 billion in the fiscal year ended June 30, 1957, to $94 billion in the year ended June 30, 1959. The deficit in the budget rose to the peacetime record—and by New Deal standards staggering—level of

$12.5 billion. In short, government spending largely turned the trick.

Now it can fairly be argued that as those in power saw the outpouring of federal funds developing, as it were in spite of themselves, they quite properly concluded that further measures, such as a tax cut, were not necessary. But it also seems true that, as in 1953-54, the conservatives were never really confronted with the agonizing necessity of having consciously to adopt measures that would substantially increase the deficit— a deficit that was already present because of the slump in receipts and the rise in spending.

In sum, we do not know from the tale of two slumps whether or not modern conservatives have adopted modern economic thought on the business cycle. We know that as individuals they differed on basic theory. We know that they were cautious about consciously —as distinct from unavoidably—adopting an "over-cure." We know that they had faith in the recuperative powers of the private economy. And we know that in fact the slumps were cured. But there remains a very legitimate doubt whether next time they would move of their own volition if the luck were not running as strongly with them. This doubt is reinforced by several extraordinary speeches by President Eisenhower in the 1958 campaign, in which he took great pride in the resistance of his administration to the "radical" approach of curing the slump of that year by masses of government spending. Of course the truth is that it *was* cured—or the cure made certain—by masses of government spending. This was, however, mostly spending that the President did not will into existence, and some of which he actively opposed. Next time, who knows?

CHAPTER TWELVE

TAMPERING WITH THE TAX

A GREAT DEAL OF THE DISCUSSION ON TAXES IN THE United States might as well be taking place on Mars. Practically everyone is convinced that our present tax structure—let alone the *level* of taxes—is all wrong and that it is only plain good sense to reform that structure. Practically everyone puts out pamphlets proving his point and testifies before Congressional committees at every opportunity. But it is mainly wasted breath. The reason is that significant shifts in the tax structure can take place only when taxes are reduced. Because of the political alignment of forces neither conservatives nor liberals really dare open up the present tax system for revision if the conditions call for no net reduction in revenue; both rightly fear that they might be the losers in those actions that raise new revenue to offset reductions elsewhere. We have seen in the discussion of the budget why no tax reduction has recently been possible, and why that condition may well last indefinitely.

But in the happy, carefree days of 1954, when the new conservative government saw the budget declining (after the Korean War) and was quite confident that it could be cut further, the great opportunity for a tax change came. The big tax revision bill of 1954 is probably the outstanding monument of the conservative regime—the one item among the "things you want to change" that was in fact accomplished. Its merits and demerits, its effects on the economy, are still being debated.

Conservatives, as we have noted, get quite excited about taxes. They feel, in the first place, that taxes are much too high for economic health—a cry of wolf that has as yet produced no actual calamities. But they also, like everyone else, feel that the "mix" of present taxes is all wrong. With considerable persuasiveness they argue that investment is the source of all our wealth and all our jobs, and that the present tax system acts as a severe deterrent to investment.

The liberal takes a decisively opposite view, also persuasive. He argues, first, that the rate of investment (mainly new plant and equipment) depends almost entirely on business assessments of the state of demand, not on the availability of funds. Thus the way to stimulate investment is to stimulate demand—chiefly consumer demand—and not to reduce the tax burden on corporations or rich investors. Businesses who feel there will be a market for the output of a new plant will find the money to build it, one way or another. In a different connection, the liberal complains bitterly that "big business" raises its investment money by using its economic power to boost prices and thereby accumulate huge profits for plowing back into new plant and equipment, instead of raising the funds from sale of new stocks or bonds. He seldom follows this complaint with a fervid plea for a reduction of the corporation income tax so that big business could set its before-tax profit target lower and thus not raise prices so much.

The position of the conservative inevitably leads him down certain paths of tax change. He wants to reduce the very-high-bracket personal tax. He wants to reduce the corporation income tax, if at all possible. He wants to liberalize the tax treatment of depreciation, meaning permission for a business to charge off more of its income for wear and tear of equipment, thus building up tax-free funds for more investment. He often expresses dismay at "double taxation of dividends"—taxation of the corporation profit and then taxation of the dividend income of the stockholder. He is for allowing small businesses to accumulate profits for expansion, for easier tax treatment of research expenditures, for reduction of the capital-gains tax. If somebody asks him where the government is to offset the revenue loss from all these changes, he frequently comes up with the idea of a general manufacturers' excise tax, which in effect is a tax on the consumer.

The liberal's position on taxes leads to equally inevitable proposals. He invariably begins by muttering about "loopholes." He means, among other things, the big tax escape for the oil and some mining industries through the "depletion" device, and the "split income" system whereby a wealthy married man can cut his tax very materially. Closing of both these "loopholes," of course, would dry up some of the investment capital that the conservatives worry about. The liberal then goes on to advocate reduction in taxes for the very lowest income groups, on grounds both of equity and stimulus to consumption and hence the economy, including investment in plant and equipment.

There was a clear-cut showdown between these two diametrically opposed philosophies in 1954. The conservative administration had a Republican Congress, and in a rare straight party fight, it won a narrow victory. The first conservative tax change in a generation had been enacted.

It will be recalled that at the beginning of 1954 there had already been a pleasant little tax reduction for practically everybody, with no issue of the tax structure. A Korean War increase of a straight 10 per cent in everyone's income tax went off, and the much detested excess profits tax for business went off at the same time. The big tax-revision bill, then, was enacted in circumstances in which the Republicans could legitimately argue that they had already given general income-tax relief, and that they were not singling out the rich or business for special benefit.

There were three main elements to the revision bill, of which the last is the one we are concerned with. First there was some general re-codification and improvement of the existing law in a technical sense. Next there was a set of useful "special" reliefs for individual income-tax payers: tax-free sickness pay, deductions for baby-sitters and additional expenses connected with the job, easier tax treatment of retirement income, etc. Finally, there were the sections aimed specifically at stimulating investment.

The most important was a change in depreciation law to allow larger deductions, for tax purposes, in the early life of a piece of equipment. There was a provision allowing small businesses to accumulate more profits without having them taxed as if they were personal income. There was more liberal deduction of research expenditures. And finally, most controversial of all, there was the provision aimed at eliminating at least a little of the "double taxation of dividends";

under it, the first $50 of dividends are tax-free and the taxpayer subtracts from his tax bill an amount equal to 4 per cent of the dividends above $50. It is important to note in light of what follows that the original proposal of the President was for a tax "credit" of 10 per cent, not 4 per cent, and the difference conceivably may be significant. The aim of this provision was not only to mitigate the alleged inequity of "double taxation"; more important, it was designed to induce a shift in corporate raising of new funds somewhat more toward stock financing and away from bond financing. The idea was that over-reliance by corporation on debt finance was potentially dangerous, threatening a wave of bankruptcies should there be another serious slump in the economy.

Well, what happened? Was investment stimulated? Was there a shift toward stock financing? To answer the last question first, the dividend provision was clearly an almost complete failure in its professed objective. Corporations are still finding at least half of their investment funds from internal sources—that is, retained earnings—and to the extent they raise new money, they have been relying on debt as much as they ever did. There was a slight increase in the proportion of stock to bond financing in 1955 and 1956, but this proportion never rose above about one-fourth and it fell back again in 1957 and 1958. There are several reasons for this, chief among them probably the fact that interest on bonds can be written off as an expense for tax purposes. Another reason may be the widely used device of "stock options" as a means of giving high executives more income without having it taxed as straight salary would be; this relatively new device has given managements a strong bias against floating new stock, which would "water the equity" and tend to drive down stock prices. It is quite likely that a few more of our citizens bought *existing* stock as a result of the new dividend credit, thus helping to run up the stock market, but the basic economic objective was not achieved. Possibly a 10 per cent credit would have done the job where a 4 per cent one could not, but this, to say the least, remains to be proved. The dividend credit, it seems, was a straight, though modest, windfall for the wealthy without any visible economic results.

As for the other changes, the events in the economy over the years following the revision bill are bafflingly inconclusive. There *was* an investment boom of notable proportions, starting about mid-1955 and lasting until mid-1957, though probably no greater, in relation to the size of the economy, than in some past periods of prosperity. Was this boom caused mainly by the tax changes or by the exuberant state of demand? Or was it caused by the astonishing proliferation of research, with its constant outflow of new products and new processes? No one can say for certain. Many liberals grasp for the best of both worlds by arguing, with dazzling inconsistency, that the 1954 tax bill caused an "excessive" investment boom, even though they have always told us that investment varies almost exclusively with the state of demand. The conservatives were delighted at the investment boom, but all through the period, with equally dazzling inconsistency, they were arguing that our tax structure, despite the changes of 1954, was still a gravely serious deterrent to investment.

Even the experience with plant and equipment expenditure after mid-1957 is not conclusive. It is clear that there was a very sharp slump, and that it was caused mainly by an equally sharp slump in demand in the economy. Indeed, between about October of 1957 and April of 1958 businesses cut back very severely on their own already reduced plans to invest, and the reason was quite obviously the recession and demand. But would the reduction have been even greater but for the 1954 tax changes?

I believe the most plausible conclusion is that the much-debated 1954 tax bill did not make a great deal of difference one way or the other. Even the conservatives admit the changes were quite modest, and they happily conclude that next time the changes must be more sweeping, particularly in the case of depreciation. The liberals would do well, probably, to stick to their last and continue to argue that investment varies with demand, not the tax structure: it is a good case.

The main tax story of the conservative regime is, of course, the story of frustration arising from the impossibility of tax reduction after the one halcyon year of 1954. But even their monument to revision has turned out not to be quite the glorious spectacle that they had hoped it would be.

CHAPTER THIRTEEN

TO AND FROM THE STATES

THE WELFARE STATE PRESENTS ITS PROBLEMS IN A nation with a federal system of government. Assuming for the moment that there is a clear necessity that certain things be done, certain new programs undertaken or old ones expanded, there are two very strong forces at work which make it unlikely that the states will do them, unaided. One is the rural domination of state legislatures. The problems with which the welfare state deals are usually urban problems, and besides, rural-dominated legislatures tend to have the traditional standpat sort of conservatism of the countryman. The second is the matter of raising the money.

To finance the cold war and such other huge and clearly federal items as veterans' benefits, interest on the debt and the farm program, to say nothing of the ordinary running of government, the federal government has largely pre-empted the income tax, the best revenue source of all. The very existence of a high federal income-tax rate imposes practical limits upon how much more the states can draw from this source. Besides, the states seem to have persuaded themselves that a major element in the decision of businesses in picking a location for a new plant is the tax structure of the states competing for that plant; hence there is a perpetual obstacle to raising taxes that affect corporations.

But there is another side to this picture, one dear to conservatives. Its heart is a strong conviction that there are decisively important benefits in the preservation of the federal system. The conservative invariably expresses horror at "centralized" power. It does no good to argue to him that Britain has managed to preserve all the essential liberties despite a highly centralized system, in which laws on everything from education standards to the location of new housing developments are made by the Parliament in London. To the American conservative, it is essential for the future liberties of Americans that power remain diffused. The term "local responsibility" crops up continually in his dia-

logue. It is a debatable position, but it is not a foolish
one.

This position has obvious results when it comes to
the question of deciding how national problems—slum
clearance, river pollution, rehabilitation of the handi-
capped, inadequate numbers of schoolrooms, a shortage
of hospitals—should be solved. The conservative's first
instinct, on political even more than economic grounds,
is to leave these problems to the states. Without thinking very deeply about the question, he finds his po-
litically derived conviction reinforced by his economic wish to reduce the *federal* budget. The more
extreme among his kind not only want to avoid taking
on any further federal responsibilities but to transfer
those already assumed to the states. Quite often the conservative does not deny the existence of the problem nor
the importance of tackling it; he merely insists that under our system the safest and wisest course is to leave
the solution to the states. We have already seen why this
approach is more likely than not to leave the problem
unsolved.

At this point it is essential to take a closer look at the
economic, as distinct from the political-philosophical,
aspect of this question. In economic terms, the only
issue is whether the nation chooses to devote more of
its total resources to public as opposed to private
purposes. A pie of a certain size must be divided. If
there are to be more slum clearance and more liberal

relief for the needy aged, there must be less autos or furniture or foreign travel or cinema patronage or even food consumption. The mechanism by which this choice is made is primarily the level of taxes. The basic statement must be qualified by a notation that the pie is always growing, so that more public services need not mean an actual *reduction* in private consumption; and by the fact that when the economy is operating at depressed levels more public services can be undertaken (through deficits in the budget) without cutting into private consumption and without being, per se, inflationary. But the original generalization still holds.

Thus when the more radical conservative fulminates about the foolishness of taking money from people in the states, sending it to Washington, wasting a bit of it, and then sending it right back to the states, he gives only half the picture. For he seldom answers the crucial question of whether he wishes the services this money provides to continue (frequently, it seems probable, he does not). If he does, then state taxes will have to rise by nearly as much as federal taxes decline; the wastage involved in the grant-in-aid system is piddling compared to the cost of the services themselves.

As we all know, American governments over time, mainly since 1932, have decided that a whole series of national problems were too pressing to be left for solution to the states or local communities. The governments of Roosevelt and Truman had no serious philosophical objection to assumption of federal responsibility, and the system of grants-in-aids—to states, local governments, local authorities, and others—proliferated. Including the highway program, they are now running at the record level of about $6.5 billion a year—and certain problems are being solved. The aged are getting reasonably adequate relief. Some slums are being cleared. Vocational education moves ahead briskly. A few rivers are being cleared, the blind are cared for, highways and hospitals and airports are being built. Almost always the states have to contribute their share, and in many programs the states actually fix the level of benefits or services. But the crucial margin of financing comes from Washington.

Most of the conservatives arriving in Washington in 1953 were resolved not to expand this system any further and, if possible, to repeal at least a part of it. Once again, the story is one of almost complete frustration. They have failed on both counts.

The most poignant episode in the story involves education, to which we shall return in a moment. But quite apart from education, the conservatives wound up expanding some old grant-in-aid programs and even starting a few new ones. For example, there is the new program of aid for construction of medical research facilities, another for helping mentally retarded children, and a new sewage plant program (this opposed

at first by the administration)—to say nothing of the
biggest of them all, the highway program. There has
been expansion in the slum-clearance program, the
hospital-building program, the vocational rehabilitation program, the program of aid for school systems
in "impacted" areas of large federal installations. In
some cases Congress went well beyond administration
recommendations, but in some others Congress failed
to adopt administration proposals. The basic reasons for
the expansion that has taken place are two: Some
problems become pressing and the conservatives had
little choice but to do, or permit Congress to do,
something about them by the device of federal legislation and federal financing; and some of the old
programs—we have already mentioned aid to dependent children—expanded under their own momentum.
Exclusive of highways, grants to state and local governments grew from $2.6 billion in the first Eisenhower
fiscal year, 1954, to $4 billion in fiscal 1959. It should
be noted that, with experience, the men in charge of
the Health, Education and Welfare Department became convinced of the value of the device of grants-
in-aid, if they were not convinced already, and were
constantly pressing for additional programs in various
problem areas.

Even they, however, believed in the principle of
terminating the federal role in older programs as new
ones became necessary. What, then, of the effort to

transfer some existing functions to the states? The effort began—typically—with the appointment of a commission. This one was called the Commission on Intergovernmental Relations, headed by Meyer Kestnbaum, and it would be difficult to find a commission whose report was so vaguely worded and so quickly forgotten (the closest parallel I can think of is another Eisenhower creation, the Fairless Commission on foreign aid). Still, the President kept bringing up this subject, which undeniably is an important one to him, and finally, in June of 1957, he made a speech at the Governors' Conference in Williamsburg, Virginia, which demanded some action. A special committee of governors and top federal officials was formed. It would perhaps be unfair to characterize their performance as another case of the mountain laboring and producing a mouse, but certainly their recommendations would scarcely shake the world. After working for a year, they came up with a program involving three items, worth less than $150 million a year in federal funds. The scheme was to have Congress pass a law transferring two of these programs—vocational education and construction of sewage plants—to exclusive state financing, and at the same time transferring part of the federal telephone excise tax to give the states more than enough money to assume the burdens. Up to this writing, Congress has shown no interest whatever in the proposal. The third item was establishment of a set of minimum required state or local expenditures in connection with natural disasters, before federal funds would be available, and this has been carried out by administrative order.

The special committee is still in existence and it may produce additional recommendations. But it has discovered that transfer to the states of the financing of the really big items—public assistance for the needy aged and dependent children is the main one—is awesomely difficult. The administration recommended a change in the formula for grants to the states in the costly program of old-age assistance (at a current level of $1 billion each year, it is much the biggest single budgetary item), and also in the formula for federal sharing of the cost of slum clearance, both aimed at reducing the federal share without reducing the total scope of the program. But in these proposals there was not even a tax transfer to sweeten the package, and the proposals have not been seriously considered by Congress. The reason is plain: congressmen, who after all represent local interests, were quite aware that a reduction in the federal share would have the almost certain result of reducing the scope of the programs involved; the states, in short, would be unable to find the money.

And now to education. This is a major item on every count. Big money is involved. The philosophical principle of local control has more meaning here than anywhere else. The national need for more finance for education, however, seems plain. With much gnashing of teeth, and after much intra-administration debate, the President finally proposed in 1956 a large program of federal aid for construction of school buildings. It would have been the biggest expansion of the grant-in-aid system in a decade and would have added more to the federal budget than all the other suggestions put together would have reduced it, at least during the four-year period of the proposed program.

The proposal became bogged down in the segregation question, in battles over the formula for assisting the different states, and in the economy drive of 1957. But a number of close observers of Congress are convinced that the defeat of the education bill in the House in the early summer of 1957 was due more than anything else to the obvious halfheartedness of the administration about the whole idea. The conservatives, in brief, were at war with themselves. The vote in the House was a defeat for a specific, and major, proposal of the President, but it was really a victory for his own underlying convictions.

The next year the administration proposed, and Congress passed, a far more modest program aimed mainly at improving the teaching of science and fostering the education of the brighter children. The bill added nearly a dozen new programs of grants-in-aid, mostly small in amount but still grants-in-aid. Out of the great soul searching on education had come a further proliferation of the hated system; more money was being taken from the people in the states, wasted a bit in Washington, and sent right back to the states again. But another problem was also being partly solved.

It should be fairly clear from the experience of conservatives in power that the question of "returning" various functions to the states (a misnomer, because most of the programs were never taken from the states in the first place, but rather started as a result of initiative in Washington) is pretty much a dead issue. Not only has the present system become so entrenched as to make a significant change impossible without severe financial strain at the state level, but also it is, after all, working rather well. We still have our liberties, and we have a quite impressive amount of "local responsibility," as anyone who wants to increase teachers' salaries or improve a sewage system or build more parking lots knows all too well. And yet we have also found a good device—an economic trick, to be sure—for getting at least some important things done.

CHAPTER FOURTEEN

FOUR RANDOM NOTES

BEFORE ROUNDING OFF OUR PICTURE WITH THE strange story of agriculture, it is necessary to touch briefly on a handful of other matters that have held the stage from time to time during the conservative regime. They are treated cursorily not because they are unimportant in themselves but because they are essentially on the fringes of economic policy as a whole. Even they, however, throw further light on the clash between conservative objectives and modern reality.

For reasons that I have never been able fully to understand, the issue of public versus private power is

capable of arousing passions in men unequaled by anything short of love or war. A liberal may be upset about
tight money or a budgetary squeeze on federal services,
but let him suspect any effort to tamper with the
Tennessee Valley Authority and his reaction is awesome.
His emotions boil, his eyes blaze, and he sees lurking
round the corner all the evils of black reaction.

Electric power is, of course, almost the only sector of
our economy where there is any pure socialism at all,
in the sense of government ownership of the means of
production. This came about mainly, though not entirely, because only the federal government had the
resources properly to develop the power potentials of
our great river valleys; there has been no serious drive
toward socialization of electric power generally—certainly not by the *federal* government. The great bulk of
our power is produced thermally rather than hydroelec-
trically, and privately rather than publicly. Fortunately
for the peace and tranquillity of the citizenry, the great
fight over the river valleys may be about over, for the
simple reason that there are almost no major river
systems left over which the issue could arise.

It is hardly necessary to say that the conservative instinct is to promote private power wherever possible—
both on grounds of general principle and for the practical reason that federal power development adds to the
budget. To the liberal, public ownership in this field
has, by the single achievement of significantly lower

electric-power costs, produced amazing results in the way of development of whole regions and improving life for individual families. There have been two major clashes over this issue during the conservative regime, and the result has been a tie—one victory for each side.

The first was Dixon-Yates. Edgar Dixon and Eugene Yates headed a pair of private-power systems that were willing to build thermal plants in part of the Tennessee Valley Authority area. The need for the plants arose because there is no more hydroelectric power to be squeezed from the area, and the TVA as a result has been forced to build more and more coal-burning steam-generating plants. Messrs. Dixon and Yates were prepared to remove this burden from TVA, and hence indirectly federal, finances. The liberals rose as one in their horror.

The liberals won the fight, in great part because the administration was so clumsy in handling it. In the end, the Republican government had to go to court with a suit to cancel its own contract on the ground that the contract had, in effect, been arrived at crookedly because of a "conflict of interests."

Out of it all came a proposal, recently enacted into law, to let the TVA become essentially self-financing. TVA may at last slip quietly out of the news.

The second clash came over Hell's Canyon, a proposed huge federal dam on the Snake River, which is perhaps the last great untapped hydroelectric power source in the country. A private-power company was willing to develop the site, but with three smaller and less expensive dams. The clash of statistics was endless and somewhat depressing. The Republicans canceled the previous administration's plans to build a federal dam, backed the grant by the Federal Power Commission of a license to the private company, and then withstood efforts year after year in Congress to reverse their decision. Now the first dam is being built and the rest of the country may in the future be spared this issue, too.

The power question came up with somewhat fewer sparks in connection, also, with rural electrification and atomic energy. The results again were a standoff. Rural electrification continues to roll along with several hundred million dollars of federal funds each year at subsidized interest rates, but the Republicans did manage to reject a few projects here and there; as a pure moneysaving device they have also proposed, unsuccessfully, a system of higher interest rates and more private financing. In the case of atomic energy, the die is not yet cast and this issue will be with us for some time. Many liberals see in atomically produced electric power the last hope for a major extension of the public-power concept, while the conservatives are equally determined to leave the development to private industry. Up to date, Congress has enacted a few more federally financed projects—mainly of a "demonstration" nature—than the administration wanted, but the big battle may be ahead of us.

Despite a remark of the President about the "socialist" nature of TVA, the conservative regime had no real intention of dismantling the public-power system that they inherited. Nor did they. But they did succeed in halting any significant extension of that system.

The essence of Republican labor policy was not in the series of relatively minor proposals for amending the Taft-Hartley Law—proposals that have not yet been enacted—but in the determination to keep Washington out of labor disputes. This was partly a matter of principle, but it had behind it the very practical, though never stated, fact that labor settlements negotiated under federal auspices are invariably liberal settlements. Labor has not yet lost a big strike that has resulted in intervention by Washington. The business community was well aware of this.

The Truman administration had intervened on numerous occasions—even to the point of temporarily seizing the struck industry—not only because it was "pro-labor" but because during most of the time it was in power the country almost literally could not afford prolonged major strikes. The period of postwar shortages had been followed very quickly by the period of Korean War mobilization.

Two things made it relatively easy for the conservatives to carry out their policy. One was that strikes could be better afforded while they were in power. Much more important was the fact that there were so few major strikes. An important reason for this was the development of the long-term contract which, though it cuts down on strikes, has tended to be achieved by major industries only at the price of exceptionally liberal, and probably inflationary, benefits.

Once during the first six years, however, there *was* a major strike. It was in the steel industry in 1956. And what happened? The government did not intervene officially, but almost certainly intervened—and decisively—unofficially. The evidence is virtually conclusive that Secretary of the Treasury Humphrey urged upon the steel companies a course that amounted to a retreat (it was, after all, an election year). The result was the most liberal steel settlement in history, a great victory for the union—and increases in steel prices during each of the three years of the contract.

I have already suggested that I feel the role of steel in the economy, and particularly in the consumer price index, is exaggerated in the public mind. But it was the very precision of the steel wage-price interaction, plus the great publicity given to the upward movements of each, that account in significant measure for the belief in the "inevitability" of inflation that has subsequently come to haunt the conservatives. What is more, this one settlement did more than anything else to spawn "administered price" and "labor cost-push" theories of inflation which were used to attack the conservative reliance on more traditional financial measures of inflation control.

As previously noted, it is my hesitant conclusion that the "wage-price spiral" is exaggerated as a "cause" of inflation, and that the root of the trouble is still excess money demand. But the steel situation alone was enough to convince a great many people, expert as well as non-expert, of the opposite. Mr. Humphrey was most emphatically hoist with his own petard.

One of the basic truths about anti-trust law that has emerged over the past decade or two is that if there are evils in "big business," anti-trust is not capable of dealing with them. The very existence of the anti-trust laws has clearly kept the basic structure of our economy far more competitive than that of any other industrialized nation; but "monopolistic competition"—situations in which an industry is dominated by a few firms—has defied efforts at correction by this or any other means. It may not be a significant evil, of course, but that is another question.

Not even the liberals have seriously charged that the Republican administration has been lax in enforcing the anti-trust laws within the scope of what *can* be accomplished. There have been criticisms of a few cases, notably the consent settlement in the telephone case.

But the total number of complaints brought and cases won has been greater during the Republican period than during a similar time span under the preceding Democratic administration. Nor has there been any shrinking from attacking the very big, as the current (and still pending) oil cases and the General Motors-DuPont case demonstrate.

The administration even incurred the wrath of the business community by proposing some changes in the law in the merger field, chiefly a change to require advance notification of proposed mergers. Congress has not yet acted, but that is scarcely the fault of the regime.

The last item in our list of random notes qualifies nicely among the list of frustrations. This is a matter of the size of the federal bureaucracy.

No article of faith was more firmly held by the business community before 1953—and perhaps still is—than that the number of federal employees is excessive. There were numerous detailed stories (many of them probably true) "proving" conclusively that time and effort was being wasted, that the job could be done by fewer people or that it was clearly superfluous. It seemed obvious that the biggest single contribution to lower budgets would be correction of this situation.

To take up the last point first, it was a complete illusion from the first. The things that make budgets big are programs, not federal personnel. Nobody has made this clearer than a member of the administration itself, after six years of experience. The then Director of the Budget, Maurice Stans, pointed out in late 1958:

> "I'd like to dispel the illusion that the federal budget can be cut severely simply by squeezing employment costs a little more. That just isn't so. Five years of close attention to this matter have produced large provable savings, but the well has just about dried up. Any future reductions in what we call 'bureaucracy' will not save billions, I assure you. . . . Besides, civilian payrolls account for only about one-seventh of our entire expenditures, and any reasonable decrease would have no major effect on the budget totals."

Yet the illusion was certainly present in the minds of many of the men who took office in early 1953. The determination to cut the "fat" from the bureaucracy was reinforced by the seemingly dangerous condition in which the budget had been found. Throughout 1953 the commonest word in Washington was "rif" (reduction in force). It seemed that the broom was sweeping with ruthless efficiency, and the figures appeared to back up this supposition. In a very short time the total of federal personnel had been reduced by some 300,000 to about 2,300,000, a reduction of no small proportions.

But the achievement was not what it had seemed. The

great bulk of this reduction came from the dismantling of price and wage and materials controls and the agencies that handled them. Elsewhere, the "rifs" were painful to individuals concerned but, in the end, piddling in total number. After the big reduction of 1953, federal employment essentially stabilized, mostly because there was no way of doing the same work with substantially fewer people.

The second Hoover Commission came and went, with vast numbers of words filed gently in quiet pigeonholes. In great part this was because this second Hoover Commission was not primarily a search for efficiency but a free pot shot at existing federal programs disliked by extreme conservatives who did not hold public office. A measure of its vast lack of importance was the fact that the President, after two years of fairly brisk activity when he came to power, gave up even submitting agency reorganization plans to Congress at about the time the Hoover Commission reported. This is not meant to imply that the search for efficiency stopped, nor that no Hoover Commission suggestions were adopted, but only that the pragmatists among the conservatives in power discovered that this was not the road to lower federal spending. By 1958 federal employment had drifted upward again to nearly 2,400,000.

The reasons why the large federal bureaucracy obviously has, and will continue to have, some built-in inefficiency range from the rules of the civil service system to the very fact of the bureaucracy's size. The great discovery of the conservatives was the ironic truth involved in all bureaucracies: they can be, and usually are, both "hard-working" and "inefficient" at the same time.

CHAPTER FIFTEEN

DISENGAGEMENT ON THE FARM

WHAT IS POSSIBLY THE BIGGEST SPECIFIC FRUSTRATION
of them all has been saved for the last. The failure of
American farm policy is certainly not limited to the
Eisenhower regime; as we shall see, the problem itself
is so appallingly difficult as to defy rational solution.
What happened when the conservatives came to power
was that all the inherent difficulties of the problem, and
the program that was invented twenty years ago to deal
with it, came into profuse bloom for the first time.

Oddly enough, except by some farmers the administration has not been much criticized for its farm policy.
Until very recently there has been no great public out-

cry to do something about the distressing situation that exists. Instead, Ezra Taft Benson is quite the idol of city dwellers, who seem to see him as a courageous knight riding into battle against an especially selfish and especially powerful interest group. Mr. Benson himself, a wizard at making phrases which have no meaning but which evoke powerful emotions, talks as if his policies were at last triumphing over evil. He is, he tells us, removing the "shackles" from agriculture and freeing the farmer from the "dead hand of bureaucracy." He is creating conditions where food and fiber can be grown for "markets, not federal warehouses." And he is doing it all without reducing farm prices.

What rot all this is! There are just as many "shackles" —in the form of acreage restrictions—on farmers today as there were when Mr. Benson took office, with the possible, and dubious, exception of corn growers. Praise be that there are. More food and fiber than ever before are being grown for federal warehouses. Although the average of *all* farm prices was higher in 1958 than before Mr. Benson began to change things, the price of nearly every individual commodity that he has tampered with is lower—and praise be for that, too.

And, for our purposes here, the worst is yet to come. We have already noted the next item briefly. While Mr. Benson was doing his unshackling and his tampering, federal expenditures on agriculture rose to the enormous total of $7.1 billion in fiscal 1959, from $2.9 billion the year the Republicans took office. We shall trace the movement of this expenditure later. The increase in farm spending has been the most important single reason for the over-all failure of the conservatives to control the budget. And yet intelligent citizens seem to believe the problem is mainly defense, or a Democratic Congress, or new programs demanded by "pressure groups."

One is annoyed at Mr. Benson, however, because of what he says—the distorted light he throws upon the picture, his claim of success where there has been failure, his references to "flexible" prices when he means lower prices—not because of what he has done. Indeed my own belief, for what it is worth, is that the direction in which he is moving may be the only hope for a solution, at some distant future date. What, then, is the problem and how did we get into such a fix?

Farm economics is a wonderland of its own. It is almost completely different from the rest of the economy in these respects:

There is a very large, in effect infinite, number of sellers.

The seller, therefore, has no control over his price. He must accept the price fixed by "the market" and his only choice is when to sell.

There is no feasible method of curbing production in a brief period of time to meet reduced demand, or of increasing it quickly to meet higher demand.

In the case of some items, demand is more or less constant and does not depend on price, certainly not in the short run. This is true, for example, of wheat.

For all of these reasons farm prices left to their own can fluctuate wildly almost from day to day, and certainly from year to year. A very small surplus can produce a very large collapse in price. Almost the only comparable example is prices on the stock market, where most of the same basic conditions hold.

Let no one underrate the potential disaster that this situation holds for the individual producer—and has in fact brought to thousands upon thousands of farm producers all through history, until governments began to intervene. Government intervention has brought exceptionally difficult problems of its own, of course, as our $6 billion expenditure only too clearly shows. But government did not intervene without reason.

To make matters even more difficult, the farm "problem" varies considerably from commodity to commodity. While the conditions described above hold for almost all commodities, sensible remedies—if they exist at all —vary from one to the other. For example, demand for wheat is "inelastic" (meaning that a lower price is unlikely to mean a bigger market, partly because a change in the price of wheat means so little in the price of bread), while the demand for oranges is relatively elastic. Cattle numbers, and hence supply, vary over a cycle that lasts years, while supplies of vegetables vary almost monthly according to weather conditions. In some cases export markets are crucial and in others they are not.

Because of all these things every government in the world, with the possible exception of the government of Monaco, has a farm problem and a farm program. Leaving out the communist world, whose difficulty has generally been that of shortage, farm programs have arisen from the perfectly proper belief of modern governments that the state has an obligation to prevent periodic suffering in any large class of citizens. Different governments have dealt with the problem through different devices, all of which have proved costly. The device adopted by the United States is supported prices, and it ranks among the costliest, and certainly the most wasteful.

The first point to make about our system is that, fortunately, it is limited in application. There are no price supports for cattle, hogs, poultry, or eggs. The whole range of fruits and vegetables is not supported, though there are schemes called "marketing agreements" under which sellers can form a sort of cartel to try to minimize price fluctuations. Most, in fact, of what human beings eat is not supported. These vast sectors of the farm economy, as a result, can and do go through periods of severe difficulty, even hardship, as the march of the cattlemen on Washington in 1954 helped to demonstrate.

The main reason why meats, fruits, and vegetables are not supported is that they are not storable, and price supports can "work" only for storable crops. The theory of price supports, as it was developed during the New Deal, is deceptively simple. A very small surplus of a crop—or even a "bunching" of marketing at one season of the year—can cause an almost bottomless drop in prices, and the reverse can happen the next year. Therefore the government would offer the farmer the opportunity of holding his crop off the market in a year or month of surplus and obtaining a government "loan" upon it. The amount of the loan would be based on a fair or "parity" price for the crop, established in relation to the prices of things farmers must buy. Later in the year, or the next year, if prices in the market were good, he could reclaim his crop and sell it, and repay the loan. If there was still a surplus that next year, he would give up the crop and the government would take it over. This government store could then be sold in years of shortage, and would be a good thing to have on hand anyway in case of emergency.

Obviously crops thus handled must be capable of storage. So the program was applied to the six "basic" crops, which were given high and mandatory supports (wheat, cotton, corn, rice, peanuts, and tobacco), to the feed grains (oats, barley, rye, grain sorghums), to storable dairy products (butter, cheese, dried milk), and to a few scattered items like rosin and honey and tung nuts. It was clear to the creators of this Frankenstein monster that there might come a need to limit production, and so there was a provision for acreage controls. So much for the problem and the way the Americans sought to solve it. What went wrong?

For many years nothing serious went wrong, and the reason was war—first World War II and then Korea. True, in both the late 1930's and late 1940's, there seemed always to be surpluses, never shortages. One good reason, of course, was that the growers had, in effect, a guaranteed market in the government. Acreage controls always seemed to come along too late. The Government-held surpluses piled up, and so did expenses. But when war came, there was an immediate worldwide demand for almost every conceivable crop, prices rose sharply, and the government could and did sell its stocks without loss and without hurting domestic prices. It is quite true, as the farm bloc used to maintain with an air of being offended by unjust criticism, that the price support program had almost no net cost for its first fifteen years. In fiscal year 1951, the program actually made money for the government, as sales far exceeded new loans.

But all this was illusion. It had already become fairly clear from the earlier experience that in normal times a guaranteed price augmented an already existing tendency toward overproduction. Less realized, because experience had been limited, was that acreage controls provide a very strong incentive toward more intensive cultivation of the permitted acreage. And not realized at all was the extraordinary capacity of new seed varieties, fertilizers, and techniques to expand yields per acre. Farming in the 1950's has gone through a technological explosion that makes industrial automation look sickly by comparison. Just to name one example, in 1958 the yield of wheat was 25.8 bushels an acre, up 56 per cent from ten years earlier.

The result, of course, was surpluses of unimaginable proportions, all "bought" by the government. Wheat had to be stored in laid-up wartime Liberty ships in the Hudson River. The Republican government desperately tried to get rid of the vast supplies by subsidizing export prices, giving relief food at home and abroad, and "selling" farm products for foreign currencies—frequently to the sharp annoyance of some of our allies who also export agricultural products. This managed roughly to stabilize stocks, at least until the huge crops of 1958, but the costs mounted. Total farm spending rose from only $650 million in fiscal 1951 to $2.9 billion in fiscal 1953, $4.9 billion in fiscal 1956, and $7.1 billion in fiscal 1959, of which all but $1 to $1.5 billion each year was price support and related expenses.

None of this was Mr. Benson's fault. I am not even persuaded that the farm price support system itself was the main culprit in bringing about the huge outpourings of crops; technology was a big factor, augmented by the fact that once capital investment on a farm has been made it is almost imperative to keep producing year after year. Still, it is clear that without price supports there would have been a total collapse in price of the crops involved and, for reasons of bankruptcy alone, an ultimate reduction of output. In any case, the system put the whole burden of absorbing the surplus on the government.

Mr. Benson's solution for the problem was in the classic conservative tradition—lower prices through lower government support levels. He drove part of his plan through Congress with great difficulty. The idea was that lower prices would expand markets and at the same time reduce incentives to produce. On the whole they did neither. As we have seen, demand for some of the main items is inflexible and markets are, in effect, not possible to expand by any reasonable price reduction. In the case of others, price cuts were apparently too small to help much (butter, for example), and in any case supplies outran even improved demand. As for the alleged effect of reducing incentives to produce, Mr. Benson's "solution," by all indications, worked in precisely the opposite direction. Confronted with lower—though still guaranteed—prices, the farmers produced all the more. True, some marginal operators gave up farming, and the farm population by the end of 1958 was the lowest in this century, far lower in proportion to the total population than ever before. But this did not nearly offset higher output by those who remained, some of whom expanded by buying the land of those who gave up.

The Secretary drove acreage restrictions to the lowest point permissible by law. And still the surpluses piled up. He tried the "soil bank," a costly device for reducing acreage still further. It expired after three years with more than $1 billion spent and the problem as bad as ever. When cotton acreage in the South was cut drastically, Southern farmers grew corn and other feed grains on the acreage, just making the feed-grain surplus worse. And lurking always in the background was the fact that an end to supports, even if it were politically possible, would have brought disaster to the farmers —numbered, unfortunately, in the hundreds of thousands—who grew the relatively few problem crops. Over twenty years we had built a machine for growing far more than we could eat or spin or export, and there was no way to dismantle the machine quickly without causing severe suffering.

Is there no way out? I am not at all sure that there is. Acreage controls certainly have not worked so far, and they have already been carried to the point where in the case of some crops they are themselves causing more hardships even than lower prices would cause, to say nothing of inefficiency. How about a completely different system? This is no place for detailed discussion, but I have seen valid and, to me, irrefutable objections raised to every idea proposed, from the "Brannan Plan" to "two-price" schemes. Subsidies as distinct from price supports—the essence of the Brannan Plan—would certainly be at least as costly as the present system and have hardly proved cheap in the countries that have tried them.

There are three longer-term trends, and one present fact, that may hold out some hope for a solution before, as Keynes once put it, we are all dead. The first is obvious—the growth of the population. The demand trend for farm products is inexorably upward. If somehow the present level of output can be prevented from increasing, eventually demand will catch up to supply.

Another is the movement away from the farms. This has the incidental effect of gradually eroding the political power of the farm bloc but, more important in the economic sense, it may be helping to accomplish the essential aim of reducing the total resources applied to agriculture, which now are clearly excessive. To the extent, however, that marginal farmers are simply selling their farms to more efficient, somewhat larger operators, there is little reduction in the most important agricultural resource of all—land.

The third is the technological explosion itself, despite the fact that it has been a major cause of the problem so far. Fortunately, it has the happy result of allowing efficient farmers—and this by no means implies "factory farms"—to operate profitably at much lower prices than ever before. It is a violation of all economic good sense that the fruits of improved technology should go entirely to the profits of the operator; some of them should go to the consumer in the form of lower prices. It is quite clear that the *efficient* modern farmer can now live very well with lower prices on those few crops that are now supported. Thus this in a sense removes some of the justification for the government price support program, at the present support levels.

The improved technology, and the reduction in the number of farms, also may eventually help to solve the "too many sellers" problem, so that producers of the problem crops can band together like the producers of citrus fruits and manipulate the timing and amount of their sales to help protect their prices, without government assistance. And finally, the one present fact that can be viewed as potentially hopeful for the future is that there are so few crops involved in the problem. At the moment, wheat is by far the most serious, with cotton, corn, and tobacco not far behind. It seems only common sense that a solution is somewhat easier if there are only a half-dozen items than if the problem applied to all of the two hundred items that are grown on our farms.

It is barely possible that if there are eventually few

enough farms, all reasonably efficient, wheat and corn and cotton can move into the category of vegetables and meats—able to operate without government price support. And the road to this utopia seems likely to be a further pressing of Mr. Benson's drive toward lower and lower price supports, to an eventual point where the support level would be a sort of "disaster floor" well below the cost of production. Only at that point, it seems likely, would reduction of price support levels succeed in the aim of inducing a significant reduction in production. Probably the only "successful" farm program—from the point of view of the budget and the taxpayer and the consumer—would be essentially no program at all.

Whether this is in fact possible I have no idea. Mr. Benson's move in this direction—a move he does his verbal best to disguise—was described to me once by a wise member of the Republican administration as a move toward "disengagement" of the government from its costly involvement in farm economics, and the huge cost of the program at present as the "price of disengagement." This is accurate in the specific as well as the general sense; for example, in order to win lower support prices for cotton, rice, and corn, Mr. Benson has been forced to permit higher acreage, and the immediate outlook is for still higher farm expenditures.

The price of disengagement is a heavy one to pay for something that is not even certain to succeed. And yet one cannot fault the conservatives for finding no other way out. The farm program was a legacy from the past and from the nature of farming economics, a part of the realities that the conservatives in power discovered to their dismay.

PART THREE

So much for the details of conservatives in action.
There remains the task of concluding this survey with
one over-all look at economic performance, an examina-
tion of what the experience of frustration produced by
way of reaction among those in power as they headed
into the final stretch of President Eisenhower's second
term, and a brief conclusion.

In doing so, we shall necessarily pick up again the
overriding theme of finance. But first, an economy, after
all, is supposed to produce a better and better life for
more and more people—to produce more and more goods
and services each year. How did the economy perform
under the conservatives?

CHAPTER SIXTEEN

ALL THIS AND STAGNATION TOO

THE SUBJECT OF "ECONOMIC GROWTH" WAS PRETTY much the preserve of professional economists until very recently. People in general who worried about economic problems thought of unemployment or prices or tax levels as measures of economic success or failure. They did not think to measure the performance of the economy by its rate of expansion. And then along came the Soviet Union.

By the end of the sixth year of the conservative regime, a comparison of growth rates between the capitalist United States and the communist Soviet Union had become common coin of conversation around the dinner table. The figures, by almost any measurement, looked bad for the U.S. Everybody accepted that a relatively more primitive economy would show a faster *percentage* rate of growth, with the same or smaller absolute advance in a given time period, than would a much bigger economy. But still, the Soviets appeared to be growing so fast that Nikita Khrushchev might even make good his boast to surpass the United States in the next couple of decades. This hardly seemed a good recommendation for the free economy as the best way of organizing society.

Congress started an inquiry into growth by the Joint Economic Committee. A Cabinet committee under Vice-President Nixon, with the loaded title of the Committee on Price Stability for Economic Growth, began exploring the same ground. Comparisons with Western Europe were made, history was checked, statistics flew thick and fast.

Measuring economic growth is a tricky business. Should it be the rise in the gross national product (total output of goods and services), adjusted for changes in prices? Should it be the rise in the "standard of living," measured perhaps by per capita after-tax income adjusted for price change? Should it be measured only after the government's share of total output is removed? Is the real test simply the rate of new investment—in plant and equipment and other types of non-residential construction—on the ground that this will determine the future rate of advance for the general economy? These are both statistical and "value" questions that it is not my function to answer. But it should be said at the outset that there is no statistically direct comparison with the Soviets, no matter what method of measurement is used. Many of the "raw" comparisons undoubtedly gave the Russians a better statistical break than they deserved.

However, it remains true that there was a strange slowing down in economic growth in the United States in the period after the Korean War—certainly by the most common measurement of growth, the "real" gross national product. This became apparent with ironic clarity when, in late 1958, the Commerce Department for the first time published gross national product figures adjusted for the rise in prices. It turned out that while the raw numbers had been rising with pleasing regularity quarter by quarter from the end of 1954 to the third quarter of 1957, much of this was illusion. The growth in G.N.P. in the "boom" years of 1956 and 1957 was mostly price rise, not physical output. For some reason, even in those years of prosperity, our rate of economic growth had fallen well below the long-term rate of about 3 per cent a year that had prevailed for as far back as the figures are available.

Of course, if the two recessions of 1953–54 and 1957–58 are thrown in, the performance looks even worse. From New Year's Day 1953 until the same day in 1959, the American economy grew by something under 1.5 per cent a year in real terms, while the Russians were growing at a rate somewhere upward of 5 per cent. And all the time our population was rising. The result was that the "real" standard of living in the United States at the end of 1958 was no higher than it had been three years earlier.

This must rank high in the list of conservative frustrations. To the extent that a conservative in power thought of economic growth, he thought in these terms: "Despite the large role of government in modern times, the American economy is still overwhelmingly a *private* economy. A free system, with profit the overriding motive, has its own built-in forces for growth, provided it is not hampered by government interference in the form of controls or excessively high taxes. Our whole history demonstrates the truth of this. Thus, to the extent government can 'promote' economic growth at all, it can best do so by keeping its own role to a minimum."

There is a great deal of truth to this analysis—certainly to the fundamental premise on which it is based. Ours *is* an overwhelmingly private economy. Economic growth, in the end, depends on the rate of investment in new productive facilities; that is, it depends on a rising *capacity* to produce (the technical term is capital formation). And, with the exception of a few power dams on large rivers or wartime aberrations such as the synthetic rubber industry, capacity in our system must be created as a result of private decisions.

The conservatives are also right in saying that, in normal circumstances, a big increase in government spending is not the way to produce a faster rate of growth. If the economy is in a slump—its present capacity underutilized—then new spending from any source, including government, produces "growth" simply by creating demand for the output of our already existing resources. The G.N.P. goes up and we in fact produce more goods and services. But in normal times —which means reasonably prosperous times—the rate of growth will depend on the rate of investment in new capacity and improved capacity. More government spending will not bring forth more output but only run up prices.

But if there was nothing inherently mistaken about the conservative analysis of growth, what went wrong when they were in power? They did remove controls. They did cut taxes once, and in a way aimed at spurring investment. Yet total output rose rapidly only in one year of their first six—the recovery year of 1955. Even if we leave out the recession periods, there remains the puzzling question of what kept our total growth rate subnormal in 1956 and 1957.

One good "answer" is that any period of two years is too short to draw conclusions on such a fundamental and complex process as economic growth. The relative stagnation of those years—usually lumped with the recessions that sandwiched them—made delicious political hay for the liberals but was not terribly impressive to the economic historians. Still, the United States was not the only country whose performance in the latter 1950's raised some fairly objective eyebrows. Britain got in a perfect intellectual sweat over the problem, with the impeccably conservative Chancellor of the Exchequer and the equally impeccable Cohen Committee both concluding that the "major economic problem of our times" was achieving a decent rate of growth without at the same time spurring on the already strong forces of inflation.

In the United States, as in Britain, conservative governments had resorted to classic weapons to restrain demand in order to stop inflation. Was "tight money," then, the main explanation for our strange slowing down? The prevailing opinion in Britain was that the measures of restraint there, centering on high interest rates, were quite definitely a major cause of the reduced rate of expansion, though possibly (depending on who was talking) worth the price. In the United States men of such divergent opinions as Sumner Slichter, Allan Sproul, and Leon Keyserling felt that restraints on demand through the tight-money weapon were a factor in slowing our growth, though they differed as in Britain as to whether that meant the restraints were a mistake.

I have suggested earlier a belief that the "bite" of tight money in the United States was probably not sufficient in the period in question to make a very large difference to either growth or inflation. Certainly it failed to deter investment in new plant and equipment. To the extent that it did exert restraint on total spending, for most of the 1955–57 period this was only proper because the economy's resources were being utilized at a high proportion of capacity. In theory, it might be shown that more spending during this period would have brought forth more output, and thus more short-run growth; but I feel the conservatives are right in their belief that it would more likely have only brought a still greater rise in prices, as indicated in earlier chapters. We were not operating at capacity during the 1955–57 boom, but we were pretty close to it.

Some of the explanation may be found in a look at the two basic "inputs" of rising total output. They are the growth in the labor force and the rise in productivity (the output of each worker per man-hour worked). The labor force during the period in question rose about in line with expectations. No trouble there. But when we look at productivity, the culprit begins to emerge.

For reasons that no one has satisfactorily explained, American productivity decided to take a rest in 1956 and 1957. Its increase in those years was apparently below the long-term rate of perhaps 2.5 per cent a year and even farther below the postwar "norm" of 3 per cent or better. The result was not only to slow down the growth in total output; it was also to add to the "cost-push" element in inflation, because the effect of wage increases on labor cost per unit of output was offset less than should be expected by rising productivity.

The subject of why productivity seems to have slowed down in the "best years" of the conservatives in power is far too complex for examination here. One common explanation is that the big boom in plant and equipment produced inevitable "bugs" in the new installations, with the result that the new facilities were actually subnormal in their efficiency in their first years. Automation, as it were, raised labor costs and reduced productivity at first, the exact opposite of its intended result. Another explanation is that we suffered in our productivity, ironically, from the boom in research. Scientists and technicians are paid but produce nothing. Employment "overhead"—represented by the rise in salaried workers while production workers remained virtually stable—increased tremendously in the post-Korean period, with the result that output for each employed worker rose less than usual.

Whatever the reason, it was not the fault of the conservatives in power. Furthermore, if the two explanations cited above have validity, the 1955–57 period laid the groundwork for a very large burst of productivity later—that is, in 1959 and 1960. The new plants will be working smoothly. The research, or some of it, will be paying off in better processes. We may be in for a period of rapid growth again.

Still, the fact remains that the conservatives—with their objective, partly achieved, of "lifting the shackles from the creative energy of a private enterprise economy"—saw that economy falter in its miraculous rise toward affluence. The faltering may well have been temporary, but still free enterprise, as it were, let the conservatives down.

CHAPTER SEVENTEEN

TRY, TRY AGAIN

IT WAS A STRANGE, ALMOST ENRAGING, THING TO BE
a conservative at the beginning of 1959.

There had been six years of Humphrey, Burgess, Anderson, Burns, Saulnier—conservatives all. There was
talk in the newspapers about the President "moving to
the right" but he was more accurate in saying he had
really been that way all along. And what had happened?

The budget had soared so high that even a Leon
Keyserling, looking ahead from January, 1953, would
not have thought it possible. The President, working
within the narrow limits of discretion given him in the
budget process, and helped by expiration of non-recur-

ring items, had reduced the budget slightly from the level of the year before, but even he was admitting that important parts of it were due inevitably to move upward. He was fighting one of the two or three most important political battles of his life to keep that upward movement in the future from being even greater. The budget had become *the* major conservative battleground—not because "pressure groups" or liberal Congresses had forced spending out of hand but because the world that the conservatives lived in for six years (new and inherited) had forced it out of hand.

The problems of managing the national debt were greater than at any time in the present century. Under a conservative regime, investors had become wary of government bonds. In the summer of 1958 there had been a speculative bubble and subsequent collapse in government bonds so great as to induce a search for corrective measures—regulative measures—by the Treasury and Federal Reserve Board. Each time a big maturity of outstanding government securities came due, men wondered whether things would turn out as they had in February of 1959, when holders of $2 billion (22 per cent) of a maturing issue refused to take an attractively priced replacement issue in exchange. One bedrock of conservatism is that the credit of the government should be preserved. It will be preserved—in the sense that the Treasury will continue to be able to pay its bills—but the nervousness of the government bond market in 1958 and 1959 was causing solid men of finance to talk of the likelihood of a "crisis" of one kind or another. This was commonplace in the days of Roosevelt; in the days of Eisenhower it was an indictment of failure.

There was talk of a "flight from the dollar." Ancient financial houses in England were writing in their annual reports of the "inability of the American government to get its finances under control" and the popular press was crowing that "the pound is now looking down upon the mighty dollar." This was the sort of thing that conservatives always said would happen if the Truman policies were carried on long enough, but it was actually happening under a conservative regime. Indeed, it was being said (with more alarmism than fact, but with some grain of truth) that the United States was "pricing itself out of world markets." This was a way of saying that, because our prices were rising faster than prices in other industrial nations, our American conservatives were less successful in preserving the value of the money than regimes abroad, some of them socialist.

Finally, one of the inherent dilemmas, mentioned earlier, of conducting an anti-inflationary debt-management policy at the same time as an anti-inflationary monetary policy was working with a vengeance. One of the main reasons why the Treasury was having trouble selling longer-term bonds was that investors figured interest rates would go higher in the future (meaning a drop in bond prices); and they figured that way in part because the Federal Reserve had made plain it was going to fight the next inflation even harder than the last. The conservatives accepted the existence of this dilemma and they believed, rightly, that the way out was not to make money easier by a different Federal Reserve policy. For if that "solution" were adopted, investor reluctance to buy bonds would have been just as great. Instead of fearing a drop in bond prices, investors would fear a big rise in the price level because of the inflationary consequences of the easier monetary policy, and so they would still be wary of fixed-interest investments such as bonds. The only way out seen by the conservatives was to kill once and for all the "inflation psychology," but that was easier said than done. In the meanwhile, they had to request of Congress a change in a forty-year-old law fixing a 4¼ per cent ceiling on the interest rate on government bonds.

The result of all these things was not only a violent reaction in the editorial page of the *Wall Street Journal* and grave warnings in the monthly newsletters of financial houses. It was a reaction among the conservatives in power themselves.

There was genuine fright in the Treasury and the Federal Reserve. There had been something of the same feeling in 1953, when George Humphrey and Joseph Dodge thought that continuation of the then existing state of affairs, and further substantial deficits, would lead to some form of disaster—ill defined but still disaster. Now there was the same sort of fright: There would be a flight from bonds and other fixed-interest investments, there would be a flight by foreigners from the dollar, inflation would turn from a creep into a gallop, taxes might have to go up and at last reach the point of serious economic harm.

The reaction took the form of grave warnings and a "battle of the budget." The Battle of the Budget in 1959 found the President strongly resisting spending proposals by the most nearly liberal Congress of his regime. His struggle, more than anything else, was a confession of failure by the first conservative regime in two decades. After five years of trying, the regime had produced (or found itself with), in fiscal 1959, the biggest budget deficit in peacetime history and the first really serious wave of "inflationary psychology" in modern times.

The only answer seemed to be more conservative than ever. Squeeze the budget—Russian challenge and depressing slums and dirty streams to the contrary notwithstanding. Stretch out the national debt at every opportunity—at the risk of even more uncertainty in the bond markets. Keep money tight and interest rates high—even with nearly five million people out of work in the winter of 1958–59. Keep trying to return functions to the states to relieve federal finance—even with the State of Michigan so tightly pinched for money that it had to appeal to large corporate taxpayers to pay in advance.

And given their view of the world and the dollar, the conservatives were right. The only cure for the disease was a stronger dose of the familiar medicine. It is not my function to say that that view was mistaken or correct, but only to try to demonstrate those elements in the real world that made the conservative experience such a frustrating one from their own viewpoint. Still, there remains the legitimate question of whether the facts of frustration should lead us to conclude that the whole conservative answer is a waste of time in the modern world. My answer may have emerged in the preceding pages, but it may be well to finish this study with a brief restatement of it.

CHAPTER EIGHTEEN

THE SOUND AND THE UNSOUND

WHAT SORT OF SHAPE WAS THE AMERICAN ECONOMY in when the first conservative regime in two decades assumed power in 1953? As the conservatives themselves saw it, it was not good. Taxes were much too high. The budget was dangerously large. The national debt was in poor condition. More and more functions seemed to be drifting into the control of the central government. There appeared a serious threat of future inflation. It was not, to use a favorite conservative phrase, a "sound" economy.

Viewed at its worst, the performance of the conservatives can be described in one glum sentence: They left the economy after six years nearly as unsound, in their terms, as they found it, and had a couple of slumps and an intervening inflation to boot. As President Eisenhower never tired of pointing out in the 1958 campaign, national well-being and the total employed were greater than ever before; but this claim, of course, could have been made by nearly every one of his predecessors in the presidency. From the left came the more meaningful claim that our economic growth had slowed materially during the conservative regime, and this was true by comparison with the earlier postwar period. In brief, it seemed a pretty sorry record, from either a liberal or a conservative viewpoint.

It is perhaps clear from the earlier chapters of this book that I feel the conservatives coming to power were more alarmed about the state of the economy than they need have been. Looking at it from what I hope is a "neutral" viewpoint, it was prosperous; standards of living were rising despite the enormous burdens imposed by hot (Korean) and cold war; partly because of reforms of the 1930's the economy appeared, and later proved, reasonably slump-resistant; Washington was not really threatening our liberties and socialism was not just around the corner; and, indeed, in 1953 there was not even an immediate inflation problem. Taxes were high, to be sure, but there had been little evidence that they were in fact preventing us in any dangerous degree from investing and creating new jobs. The budget was big and so was the national debt, but we were living in fair comfort with both.

And yet the inflation of 1956–57 showed that the economy did have at least one serious unresolved difficulty. While this inflation itself certainly did not ruin us, and while the slump that followed it was brief, there remains a serious question whether the American economy can live well—continuously well—without solving the problem of inflation. To the extent that the conservative description of the economy as "unsound" meant that its condition was potentially inflationary, their fears were warranted. Viewed in that light, too, their record may not appear quite so unsuccessful.

For who is to say how much worse our inflation might have been but for tight money, the squeeze on some parts of the budget to mitigate the uncontrollable increases in other parts, the efforts to fund the debt? The stress throughout this book has been on the discovery by the conservatives of why living fully in the conservative way in the modern world is so difficult as to be nearly impossible. But the Republican regime of the middle 1950's undoubtedly kept the shape of things more conservative than they otherwise would have been. If the classical theory of inflation—excessive demand —has validity, as I am convinced it does, then these efforts bore some fruit. The price level would be higher now but for the fact that conservatives were in power.

And yet the irony, as we have suggested, is that the

failure of a conservative regime to stop the price rise altogether—associated with the failure to control the budget, solve the farm problem, stretch out the national debt—has greatly strengthened the conviction that more inflation is inevitable; and this conviction in turn may help to speed the process. The conviction, showing up so strongly in the stock market through the last half of 1958 and early 1959, has been reinforced by the comparative ease with which the economy rallied from the two slumps that occurred during the same period.

The cynicism about the future of the price level would appear warranted from the story of the conservatives in power. And that is the true tragedy. For nothing that the "real world" did to frustrate conservative performance renders invalid conservative objectives. This book is the story of why the objectives are far more difficult to achieve than was realized in 1952, but the story does not warrant the conclusion that they cannot ever be achieved, at least in great part. Indeed, they probably *were* achieved in part, and with a better knowledge of the realities they may be even more closely approached in the future. We shall all be the losers if conservative objectives become discredited because we now know some of the obstacles to conservative performance.